Each Day a Gift

A Gratitude Devotional for Women

A Gratitude Devotional for Women

Each Day a Gift

90 Devotions
to Make a Habit of
Praise and Thanks

Sabrina U. Lawton

ALTHEA
PRESS

Interior and Cover Designer: Emma Hall
Production Editor: Erum Khan
Author photo © Lydia Carlis, Eyemagination Imaging

ISBN: Print 978-1-64152-321-9 | eBook 978-1-64152-322-6

In dedication to you,

for your loving

devotion to

God

Contents

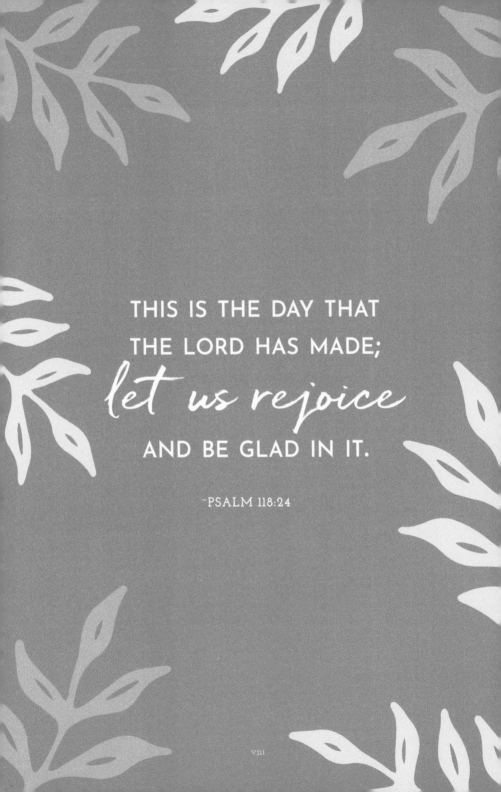

THIS IS THE DAY THAT
THE LORD HAS MADE;
let us rejoice
AND BE GLAD IN IT.

~PSALM 118:24

Introduction

What powerful words: "This is the day that the Lord has made; let us rejoice and be glad in it." What does rejoicing look like to you? Can you imagine the bright lights, your smile, the music, and jubilant dancing?

God asks us to greet each day in our own celebratory way and to open the doors of grateful acceptance that allow us to perceive his hand in all circumstances. Yet it's so very easy for us to get caught up and focus mostly on the trials of our busy and often hectic lives. We desperately want to join the celebration, but how can we if we aren't even able to notice it?

In turning to this devotional, you're choosing to notice the celebration by setting a daily, divine appointment with God. If you're the type of person who makes to-do lists, why not put time with this devotional as the first thing on your list each day? There is truly nothing that compares with the soul-nourishment you'll receive from spending even just a few minutes of private time focused on God.

While I'm certain that you, like me, have an unwavering love for God in your heart, many of us wait to begin an urgent conversation with him until the going gets tough. But if we don't regularly reflect on the incredible things God has done for us, we risk only turning to him when we want an escape route from our troubles. By comprehending his caring and generous nature on a daily basis, and regularly praising him for it, we are more likely to remain hopeful when we inevitably face situations that challenge our faith. If we can cultivate closeness in times of plenty, imagine how much more powerful our connection with him will be in times of turmoil. Indeed, adopting a steadfast attitude of gratitude is invaluable to helping us cope with everything from everyday disappointments to physical and spiritual crises.

For many years, I felt the heavy weight of the many challenges in my life. As a fatherless child, I suffered from violence and abuse. My mother did the best she could to raise me, yet she was only a teenager when I was born; her resources were limited. Feelings of loneliness, depression, and self-doubt caused me to fall into a cycle of unhealthy relationships. I sensed there was a God-shaped hole in my heart, but it wasn't until I hit rock-bottom and reached upward towards God that the redeeming grace of his presence entered my life and made me whole again.

Looking back, it might appear that I have very little to be grateful for, but I am writing this book on the transformative power of gratitude for two reasons.

- God's forgiveness, grace, mercy, and love helped me to transcend my painful past.
- God healed me by showing me how I could grow spiritually by being grateful for the very experiences that had broken my heart.

God knows not only the number of our days, but what we need to grow in faith and love. Each day is indeed the day that the Lord has made for me, and for you!

My abrupt awakening happened after I got into a serious car accident that changed the trajectory of my entire life. So debilitating were the physical effects that I was forced into silence and stillness. One day I found myself on my knees in the center of my family room, my face planted in the ground. I didn't speak a word but mentally sent a desperate and agonizing prayer to God: "Everything I think I am, I give it to you! Everything the world has taught me about my value as a woman, I give it to you! I am empty now. You will have to show me who I am."

As you can imagine, that was the first time I was still enough to hear God's own still, small voice. God revealed to me that only through love could I evolve spiritually, and heal emotionally and physically. After that day, I immersed myself in study of the Bible—which I affectionately refer to as **B**asic **I**nstructions **B**efore **L**eaving **E**arth—and learned everything I could about love through the teachings of Jesus Christ. I am a living witness that "All things work together for the good of those who serve the Lord!"

Today I am eternally grateful for my God-centered marriage and my two lovely children, though the path I took to this present moment was indeed rocky. I am also deeply grateful for the experience of the majesty of God's presence in my life each day. I know too well that God holds the key. In turn, I am eager to share with you just how you can deepen your faith and trust through daily praise, allowing you to see each day as a gift, regardless of your experience.

If you are turning to this devotional for general upliftment, I hope my passion and joy for the Lord help spark and deepen the same in you. If you are drawn to this devotional because you have suffered deeply and believe that gratitude might be the only way out of your own pain, know that you have a sister in me. While everyone benefits from turning to gratitude, the practice of gratitude can be especially powerful for those of us who have experienced real trauma. In Christ we are a new creation! God can turn all evil into good. By thanking God in advance, I've discovered the power in my pain, as well as the deeper purpose for both my setbacks and breakthroughs. I am grateful to be your guide as you make each day a gift of gratitude.

To get the most out of the next 90 days, be intentional about having an attitude of gratitude. Each devotion includes a prayer and a guided reflection to help you gain a new perspective on your life, right where you are, right now. Through these readings, my hope is that you will feel ever more deeply in your heart and soul that his love for you is boundless and that what he sends to you is exactly what you need. How much more do you think you will have to be thankful for when you start thanking God for what you have?

Devotions

Day 1

Sacred Self-Care

After all, no one ever hated their own body, but they feed and care for their body, just as Christ does the church—for we are members of his body.

~EPHESIANS 5:29–30 NIV

As women, we carry many titles. We are daughters, sisters, girlfriends, wives, mothers, aunts: We are caregivers. We have a natural drive to love, nurture, defend, and care for the people around us. We want our kids to look nice and shiny on their way out the door for school; we want good, healthy lunches made; and we'd love it if our partner could return to a warm home and a good meal.

These days, many of us have careers, too—the juggle is real! We attempt to "do it all" for everyone, and of course this can cause us to feel exhausted and overwhelmed. But what if the real reason you're struggling to care for others is because you haven't made caring for *you* a priority? Caring for yourself is not a selfish thing. You cannot fill anyone up from an empty cup. Only when you are able to truly care for yourself will you have enough to be able to give from your overflow.

How much time do you spend each day caring for *your* body and feeding *your* soul? Have you reflected lately on anything beyond a mirror? Sacred self-care is not about going on a mini shopping spree or getting a mani-pedi. Sacred self-care is about loving yourself enough to connect daily with God in you.

Be intentional about carving out a few minutes each day—just as you are doing with this book—to have regular conversations with God. He wants you to love yourself as he loves you, and he wants to be close to you. When you make a habit of filling up on spiritual food, you will receive insight, wisdom, and understanding about how to love yourself, and those around you, even more!

Heavenly Creator, I am grateful to know that to love me first is to love you first. Help me treat my body as a sacred part of the Body of Christ. Help me prepare my temple to reflect your image and likeness in the earth.

Today, I am grateful to love myself as God loves me by creating the following weekly sacred self-care regimen:

....

....

....

....

....

Day 2

God in Nature

"But ask the beasts, and they will teach you; the birds
of the heavens, and they will tell you; or the
bushes of the earth, and they will teach you;
and the fish of the sea will declare to you."

~JOB 12:7–8

Never doubt that you are on a beautiful journey of seeking and finding God in your life. Just ask the beasts of the fields, the birds of the air, the clouds in the heavens, the fish of the sea. They will tell you, teach you, show you the magnificence of God in their glory, right here on Earth! These beautiful creatures hold the keys to the paradise you seek. Stop and take in the behaviors of the animals, the scents and sensations of the breeze passing through your lips. Be still with the not-so-stillness of a tree, and listen for the sounds of life that emit from within its branches.

We all experience disappointments and challenges, joys and opportunities. Whether sliding on a low or riding a high, it is all too easy to get caught up in the emotions of our daily lives. We must take care to remind ourselves that God is ready right now, in this very moment, for us not only to accept our circumstances but transcend them by experiencing the kingdom of heaven in our midst.

If Mother Nature is not God, then who is she? Make it a practice to listen to the teachings of the beautiful, vast nature of the God that is all around and apply them to your life. The ants enjoy their work of gathering and storing food, the birds play in the sky while appreciating the view, the dogs do not remember the treat they didn't receive yesterday. All of nature is naturally *being* in the here and now. Forget yesterday. Do not imagine tomorrow. Today, this moment, enjoy *being* with God.

Heavenly Creator, thank you for speaking to me through the beauty and being of nature. Like the sea and the ocean, teach me to flow with the tides of my life. Help me ride the waves, knowing your hand is in the midst of it all.

Today, I am grateful to commit to spending few moments in nature, at the following time, and in the following location:

....

....

....

....

....

Day 3
Perfect Peace

You will keep in perfect peace all who trust in you,
all whose thoughts are fixed on you!

~ISAIAH 26:3 NLT

To anything you are going through, from credit card debt to family drama, say "Amen." If you are saying "Amen," you are praying. If you are praying, that means you are fixed on God for your peace while you await his direction. Whenever we get into tough situations, it's easy to let go of God's hand and take matters into our own.

We might instantly begin to seek the advice of others while also racking our brains to find the solution. Certainly, coming up with a plan is a good idea, but what if God wants us to turn to him right away and continually? Thankfully, when we run to God and lay our problems at his feet, he assumes them, and we can release them. Only in those moments of true surrender can we begin to cultivate the perfect peace that will see us through.

At one of the proudest moments in my life, I recall feeling betrayed by a family member. She spoke very negatively about something I had poured my sweat and tears into. She basically told me that my work was in vain and also made accusations against me. I was shocked to hear the things that came out of her mouth! The pain cut deep, and yet I knew in that moment I had a choice: either allow that person to steal my joy or give the hurt to God.

I decided to fix my thoughts on God's word. I chose not to try to explain myself or fight back. I prayed for the person and proceeded in peace to walk right through the doors to whatever lay ahead as my destiny.

Let no one steal your peace—not your neighbor, your boss, your parents, your sister, your brother. Fix your thoughts on Jesus, and you will be filled with a peace that surpasses all understanding.

Heavenly Creator, thank you for keeping me in your perfect peace. Help me hand over to you anyone who threatens to steal my peace. I am grateful that this is not my battle to fight. I pray a prayer of peace and blessings for others as I shift my focus onto you.

Today, it is with a heart of gratitude that I stay in perfect peace by giving these people to God:

....

....

....

....

....

To Stay or Walk Away?

Do not be misled: "Bad company corrupts
good character."

~1 CORINTHIANS 15:33 NIV

I struggled for over a decade in a relationship with my son's father. After years of effort and pain, we went our separate ways. As I reflected, it became clear that I had stayed so long because we shared a child, and I was terrified of starting my life all over again. I'd grown up in the relationship—I was only 16 when we first met—and single adulthood was foreign to me! Yet I knew that if I remained in the relationship, I would not become who God had created me to be.

My ex was a heavy smoker with no intentions of quitting; a healthy lifestyle was of great importance to me. He had trouble actualizing his ambitions; I imagined how I could do my part to change the world. While he wasn't a bad person, he became bad company for me. And truthfully, I had not behaved like an angel in our relationship; I was no longer good company for him either.

After our marriage ended, I was able to reflect on the gifts that the relationship had blessed me with—namely, the love and protection of the father figure I'd never had during the most vulnerable years of my life. As a consequence of childhood molestation and other factors, I had been troubled during my teenage years and engaged in promiscuous behavior. I can see how much more trouble I would have gotten into had I been single, wild, and free during those years. I am grateful for our beautiful son, who is a loving and kind young adult. Although my ex and I did not work out in romantic love, I know that God chose this man to be my son's father. It also is crystal clear that there was a time to stay and a time to walk away.

In this life, you will encounter well-intentioned people who seemingly hold you back from all that God has in store for you. They might be romantic partners, friends, or even family members. I understand the emotional strongholds these relationships can have, but place your allegiance in God before man. Move forward with a heart of peace and forgiveness.

Heavenly Creator, thank you for giving me the courage to walk away from relationships that do not serve my highest good. I pray for their own highest good as I walk away with good reason, whether for a season or a lifetime.

I am grateful for the following lessons I've learned and blessings I've received through these relationships:

....

....

....

....

....

Day 5

You Are Perfectly Imperfect!

*Then God said, "Let us make human beings
in our image, to be like us."*

~GENESIS 1:26 NLT

If you are anything like most women, you spend time picking apart what you look like. You may want to be smaller, taller, or more "attractive" in one way or another. But wait! This could not be what God had in mind when he created us in his own image and likeness. On the contrary, it is Satan who distorts God's standards of beauty and spreads the lie of vanity.

For much of my life, I felt unworthy. I tried to conceal my feelings by dressing up and presenting a pretty package on the outside, to hide what was on the inside. I began to believe that my age would cause me to become unwanted. When my vain imaginings became too painful, I decided to put my beliefs about my value on pause and paint a more perfect picture in my mind.

Women who have a true impact on our world—women such as Mother Teresa, Oprah Winfrey, Michelle Obama, Rosa Parks, and Malala Yousafzai—have a beauty that far transcends appearance. Their gifts to the evolution of humanity have nothing to do with their looks.

Thankfully, what God considers beautiful is very different from what the world leads us to believe is beautiful. Man looks on the flesh; God looks on the spirit. It is that simple, but I know it can be very hard to live by.

I decided to get unbound by the flesh by challenging myself: Each time I became hyper-focused on what I looked like, I would tell myself I was serving Satan's desire for my life, not God's. I made a decision to stop worrying about my age, my hair, and the stretch marks I affectionately call my "stripes of motherhood." I resolved that each time I had a negative thought, I would declare, "I am made in the image and likeness of God!" This affirmation has allowed me to find gratitude in the fact that God made me perfectly as I am and that I should embrace his wisdom as it shines brightly and uniquely through me. I am God's beautiful work of art!

Heavenly Creator, thank you for making me in your likeness! I'm grateful that you created me with such great intention, from the hairs on my head to the soles of my feet. Help me honor my body, mind, heart, and soul—the most beautiful parts of me.

Today, I am grateful to see the following parts of me in a whole new and beautiful way:

....

....

....

....

....

Day 6

Give Thanks

*Give thanks in all circumstances; for this is the
will of God in Christ Jesus for you.*

~1 THESSALONIANS 5:18

Did you receive what God said? Give thanks in *all* circumstances, for it is God's will. If you are a parent, you know how quickly life can get turned upside down.

When my son was 14, he began to lash out. Yet I knew there were underlying reasons. My divorce from his father had a deeply negative impact. The strain of moving from house to house and being caught in the middle of the constant tension had taken an emotional toll.

One day, I was prompted in the Spirit to sit down very intentionally with my son. I took him to a lakefront, sang him a song, and asked if he would be open to moving into my house on a full-time basis. Thankfully, he agreed. As time went on, we prayed together and shared biblical truths regularly. While the journey to his healing was bumpy, God saw us through!

I asked my son to forgive me for my role in the disruption of his life. In return, he expressed the feelings he had experienced during the divorce. He also developed a wonderful relationship with my second husband and our daughter (his half sister), and finally he decided he wanted to turn his life around. Our son graduated from high school with honors and went to college; more importantly, he healed as he began to view his childhood wounds with deeper wisdom and understanding.

Worry is profoundly burdensome. In the course of worrying about the unknown or what we dread may come, we can create fearful scenarios in our minds. The best thing you can do to maintain your peace is give thanks in advance for what God will do in your life or in the lives of those you love. We often ask ourselves, "What would Jesus do?" Let us remember to thank

God for all our circumstances, as Jesus did, even as we try to understand whether our role in the moment is to carry or support, and as we determine when to release and let go. This is a quick way to access the peace of heaven, especially during times when life might feel like a living hell.

Heavenly Creator, I'm grateful to release into your loving arms the fate of the people, places, and things I have held attachments to. Help me give thanks in all circumstances, for the best way to serve the people I love is by maintaining my own peace.

Today, I release to you, and give thanks in advance for, the resolution to the following circumstance:

....

....

....

....

....

Day 7

Take Up Your Bed and Walk

"Which is easier, to say to the paralytic, 'Your sins are forgiven,' or to say, 'Rise, take up your bed and walk'?"

~MARK 2:9

This verse refers to a Bible story in which Jesus healed a man who'd suffered from paralysis. Imagine that you are the one unable to move. Your paralysis can be physical or emotional. Who hasn't been in a situation that caused us to be so overwhelmed that we just froze in fear and did nothing at all?

Like the paralyzed man, have you ever laid in bed all day (or felt like it)? After a period of self-pity, you may start to wonder if you are worthy of feeling better. Jesus first told the man, "Your sins are forgiven," but that didn't make him move. In the same way, we may say we know that we are forgiven by God, but do we really believe it if we cannot forgive ourselves and move on with our lives? Jesus is so amazing that he overlooks our own disbelief that our sins could be forgiven and goes on to instruct, "Take up your bed and walk." He knows we need the push of proving his words. Only when the paralyzed man got up and walked did he know he was healed.

I began to think through the sins that had caused me to be confined to my bed, in the darkness of depression for years. I wanted desperately to move forward, and I began to realize my own thoughts were deceiving me, so I followed Jesus's command, got myself up both literally and figuratively, and trained my eyes on what lay ahead. That is when my healing began.

God created you with the ability to get up and walk toward the light of the Son, carrying with you everything you think has caused sickness in your body, mind, and soul. When you take up your bed and walk, you will find that not only are your sins forgiven and your errors overlooked, but your life—sin and all—will be used as a walking testament of God's unfailing love, mercy, and grace.

Heavenly Creator, thank you for calling me to come to you as I am. I am grateful for your love, forgiveness, mercy, and grace. Help me lift my bed off the ground, heavy as it may be, and walk into my destiny with courage and faith.

Today, it is with faith and gratitude for God's mercy that I take up my bed and walk by doing the following:

....

....

....

....

....

Act on Your Dreams

"God is not human, that he should lie, not a human being, that he should change his mind. Does he speak and then not act? Does he promise and not fulfill?"

~NUMBERS 23:19 NIV

Have you been dreaming of something big? Perhaps you want to expand your family, ask for a raise, or consider moving to a new town. However, following through can be downright terrifying! It requires us to travel through uncharted territory. Your mind may swirl with questions like, "What if it doesn't work?" When doubts creep in, instead ask yourself, "What if it *does* work?" God gave you the dream, and God does not lie or change his mind.

My dream might never have been realized if it weren't for a car accident. As a result of the crash, the right side of my jaw, neck, and shoulder locked up so intensely that I suffered migraines, poor range of motion, and chronic inflammation on the right side of my body. Unable to continue to work, I took a six-month leave of absence.

Home alone with zero distractions, I had no choice but to be present in my life and take inventory. Though I had a successful career, all I could think about were the messes in the corners of my life that I'd long ignored. In a desperate cry, I asked God not to fix those messes but rather to "show me who I *really* am." To my surprise, I received in response one word: *evolve*. God continued, "If you are going to evolve, if the world is going to evolve, you must love . . . Look, the word *love* is in *evolve*."

I studied all I could about love, and my emotional healing followed. I felt called to share this understanding with others, and through that mission I founded my organization, Evolve to Love. Even as I pressed forward, I struggled with doubts and insecurities. But God planted the seed, and I believed, so I acted. The testimonials of those whom I have served in ministry convince me that I indeed followed the path God laid for me.

Instead of worrying if your dream is possible or questioning how you could accomplish it, send a prayer of gratitude to God, knowing that he put the dream in your heart and chose *you* to bring it to pass.

Heavenly Creator, help me put complete trust and faith in you regarding the fulfillment of my dreams. Reaching my destiny will be a tumultuous journey; nevertheless, I will act on my dreams as a demonstration of faith and belief.

I am grateful that these promises will come to pass in God's perfect will and God's perfect way:

....

....

....

....

....

Day 9

Faith over Fear

When I am afraid, I put my trust in you.
In God, whose word I praise, in God I trust;
I shall not be afraid. What can flesh do to me?

~PSALM 56:3–4

Can you imagine where our world would be if more people put their faith in God when life got really rough? It's easy for us to praise God when everything is sunshine and rainbows, but what about when you experience a health scare or have to say goodbye to someone you can't imagine living without? Fear can paralyze you and render you immobile, preventing you from fulfilling your destiny, but you can have power over fear when you realize that most of the things you're anxious about do not actually ever come true.

Think back to a time when you were afraid of something—a health diagnosis, a job change, or a messy breakup. Now consider the reality of the aftermath. Where are you now? Were the sadness, fear, and stress you felt about the situation justified? Save yourself undue emotional pain, and activate your faith in order to overcome fear.

Faith does not require you to *feel* any particular way. You can engage your faith and praise God regardless of how you feel. Faith simply asks that you overlook feelings of sadness, anger, and fear so you can turn instead toward the light that comes from praising, trusting, understanding, and doing God's will.

When you are sad, faith can motivate you to get out of bed while fear encourages you to bury your head under the covers. When you are afraid about a diagnosis, faith will prompt you to trust God and declare, "God's got this," while fear will prompt you to dwell on and languish in your illness and related negative feelings. Let's be clear: Your healing and your ability to praise God in the midst of it all will always come more powerfully by way of faith over fear.

Heavenly Creator, thank you for the miraculous spirit and healing found in faith! I trust that even in sickness, you know what is best for me. I will praise you fearlessly, trusting your will over my life.

Today, I am grateful to praise God as I choose faith over fear in these areas of my life:

You Are God's Temple

*Do you not know that you are God's temple
and that God's Spirit dwells in you?*

~1 CORINTHIANS 3:16

You are a woman, and you are God's temple. In our faith, we often refer
to God with masculine pronouns, so it may be difficult to believe that God
could have any feminine qualities. Many doctrines teach of a God who is
punishing, authoritative, and very masculine in nature while the feminine
qualities of God, such as our ability to create life, nurture others, and have
compassion, are classified as merely earth-realm functions.

Television programming and societal norms have placed the value
of women in one-size-fits-all boxes called physical beauty, motherhood,
and other forms of subservience. This has caused many women to feel
disconnected from our own divinity, making it very difficult for us to
love ourselves as we are.

God needs you to be a part of the paradigm shift! You, standing in
your feminine power, are *exactly* what is needed to bring about the balance
of peace, love, and harmony in our world. God made all humankind
in his image and likeness, so look to your soul. What do you see? Look
beyond your perceived flaws, and recognize what is undeniably good
about you. Embrace those qualities, thank God for them, and use those
gifts to love yourself, and you will naturally love others more fully.

If a man comes and finds your temple beautiful on the outside,
yet discovers when he enters that it is devoid of the treasures of
wisdom and understanding, he will take what little treasure you have
and leave your temple even more empty than it was before. If a good

man finds that you possess within you the treasures of self-love and self-confidence, and you walk in the authority of the Holy Spirit within, he will be drawn to remain with you.

Heavenly Creator, thank you for creating me in your image, and help me remember that my body is a glorious temple of God, not a nicely decorated empty shell. It becomes even more beautiful as I age and gather wisdom. Give me the courage to love myself by allowing only those who honor your Spirit within me to enter into my sacred temple. In order to make room for my treasures of wisdom and love, help me keep this temple sacred by letting go of relationships that do not bring me closer to your purpose for my life.

Today, I am grateful to honor my temple as a glorious embodiment of God by recognizing who adds to or detracts from your holiness within me:

....

....

....

....

....

Day 11

Pace over Haste

Desire without knowledge is not good—how much
more will hasty feet miss the way!

~PROVERBS 19:2 NIV

Today you have decided to put God first. This is evident by very virtue of
the fact that you have picked up this devotional to lean in to God's word
for your life. The question now is, how will you proceed with the rest of
your day? When you put down this devotional, will you resume your pace
and run out in haste to get to work, drop off the kids at school, clean your
home, or swiftly check off the next box on your to-do list? I know what
it feels like to believe your life has become nothing more than a string of
laborious tasks. This lifestyle had me completely stressed out, anxious,
and exhausted!

When living a hurried life, I would do things like drive too fast and
get speeding tickets. I even got into a few small fender benders. Other
times, I was in such a hurry to leave the house that I forgot something
important and ended up having to backtrack and get what I had left
behind. Just think of all the time we lose when we race through life this
way. Surely God did not create the miraculous sky, trees, and flowers, and
children's beautiful faces, just for us to race past them all without much
thought day after day.

I began to ask myself, "Why am I always in a hurry to get nowhere?"
I heard the voice say, "Many in your family are rushed. This is a learned
behavior, and I have given you grace—now, stop." Wow! Just look at the
simplicity and grace of God. When you take a moment to slow down
and be with God each day in prayer and supplication, you give yourself

the gift of experiencing God in all things. When your feet are swift, you are likely to miss God's way. Before you take your next step, I encourage you to practice the acronym STOP: **S**top. **T**ake a deep breath. **O**bserve the situation. **P**roceed with thanksgiving—and acknowledge everything that is good in God's world all around you.

Heavenly Creator, thank you for being patient with me as I learn to be patient with myself. Today, I will slow my pace and become present in everything I do so that I can experience you.

Today, I am grateful for the ability to pace myself with peace and presence during these activities:

....

....

....

....

....

Day 12

Your Child, God's Creation

For you formed my inward parts; you knitted me together in my mother's womb. I praise you, for I am fearfully and wonderfully made. Wonderful are your works; my soul knows it very well.

~PSALM 139:13–14

When we consider the things in life for which we are grateful, children top the list for many of us, even if we are not parents. If you are a parent, however, you know the strain of constant worry. You can't imagine your child going through some of the things you went through, and perhaps you wonder if you will be a good enough parent to protect your child from emotional, physical, and spiritual distress. I know how debilitating it can be to helplessly watch your child deal with sadness, depression, or self-destructive behaviors!

My son was just 16 when he went against my will and got tattooed. The ink was dry, and the tattoos were permanent. I had no choice but to accept that every time I saw my son, I would also see a sleeve of tattoos along his forearm. I took it to God in prayer, and God directed me to this: "Your eyes saw my unformed substance; in your book were written, every one of them, the days that were formed for me, when as yet there was none of them" (Psalm 139:16). When I embraced the fact that, while my son was birthed through me, he is ultimately God's creation with a calling all his own, I was able to see my son's tattoos through the lens of love, acceptance, and yes, even gratitude.

His tattoos actually read "Son of God," with a beautiful backdrop of pyramids and a lion with green eyes like his. He chose to grace his other arm with just one thing: the name of his little sister, whom he loves dearly. When I surrendered my son to God, only then was I able to see the beauty in my son's choices. He is now 22. He is very responsible and has a good job, he is vegan, he attends college, and he has big dreams! What more can a parent ask for?

Heavenly Creator, I pray for the wisdom and understanding to teach my child in the way they should go. When I have a hard time understanding my child's decisions, I will surrender my child to you, trusting that this is a part of my child's destiny as they find their footing on their soul's path to you.

Today, it is with gratitude that I release the following worries and concerns about my child to God:

....

....

....

....

....

Count It All Joy

Dear brothers and sisters, when troubles of any kind come
your way, consider it an opportunity for great joy.
For you know that when your faith is tested, your
endurance has a chance to grow. So let it grow,
for when your endurance is fully developed, you
will be perfect and complete, needing nothing.

~JAMES 1:2–4 NLT

Many of us will experience challenges in this life. I am certainly no exception. I spent far too much time and energy looking for love in all the wrong places. This caused great trouble in my life. I was intimate with men who didn't deserve me. I struggled with depression because it seemed that my life was crumbling down in every direction, and all I ever really wanted was to feel loved. Now that I have transcended that pain, I can look back and know with certainty that it was actually those painful, dark nights of the soul that led me to God's destiny, which was to stop seeking the approval of men, start receiving the love of God, and help other women do the same.

Through my organization, I facilitate retreats designed to help women to evolve from walking in the flesh to walking in the Spirit. As a natural by-product of this process, many of those women go on to attract the spiritual men God has in store for their lives. I would have never known my calling to help others understand the value of keeping your sexy sacred had I not personally experienced the pain caused by low self-esteem, vanity, and sexual immorality. Thankfully, we can count it all joy! What hell meant for evil, God wants to use for your good!

Whenever things don't go as planned, instead of resisting or asking why, consider that God's plan reaches far beyond what your eyes can see. Choose to see every adversity, conflict, and disappointment as an experience designed to help you build spiritual endurance. When you allow your faith and endurance to grow, you'll gain the ability to build strong foundational pillars in every area of your life, and you will need for nothing.

Heavenly Creator, thank you for my adversities, failures, and disappointments. I count it all joy, for I know these things are preparing me for my divine destiny. I choose to see every perceived defeat through the lens of faith, hope, and love. May your perfect will be done.

Today, I am grateful to count it all joy, knowing my path is being perfected through these experiences:

....

....

....

....

....

Simple Abundance

*Those who trust in their riches will fall, but the righteous
will thrive like a green leaf.*

~PROVERBS 11:28 NIV

Abundance is everywhere around you. Try counting the number of leaves
on the trees or the blades of grass, and you will not find their end. What
about the number of raindrops when it rains? And what of the grains of
sand? Whether it be a downpour or a light sprinkle, there is still an abundance! The point is, God does not think small. God has stores of abundance
for us, and there is more than enough to circle the earth several times
over and back! Ironically, we live in a world where there is great disparity
between the rich and the poor. This is because too many of us are trusting
in the things our riches will get us and not trusting in God.

Certainly, you can be wealthy and know God. Likewise, you can live
in poverty and know God. In either case, abundance is not about all that
we have as much as all that awaits us through salvation in Christ. For
where your treasure lies, there your heart will be also.

In God's economy, righteousness is the mathematical equation for
true and simple abundance. When the leaves of the trees become exces-
sively abundant in the summertime, they *fall*, giving nourishment to the
soil below. Through the winter, the trees experience nakedness, or the
appearance of having "less than," and they do it all without resistance!
By simply allowing the spring to come in its due time, the tree is grace-
fully clothed again, and the cycle of thriving life continues.

When it comes to living a life of abundance, instead of seeking to thrive in riches, seek to thrive in righteousness and purpose; and just like the tree, when you stand firmly wherever you are planted and remain in a state of gratitude, you are certain to experience the *simple abundance of the soul* that comes from trusting God in every cycle of your life.

Heavenly Creator, today I choose to look upon the simple abundance all around me and acknowledge that you do no small thing. I thank you for helping me see that just as all things in nature thrive by living out their purpose, so, too, will I thrive when I focus not on riches but on your purpose for my life.

Today, I am grateful for the abundance that is mine when I focus on righteousness in these areas of my life:

....

....

....

....

....

"THE SPIRIT OF GOD
HAS MADE ME, AND THE
BREATH OF THE ALMIGHTY

gives me life."

~JOB 33:4

Day 15
Just Breathe

Living in this fast-paced world can have your mind swirling with its demands. There are probably a million things on your list of things to do, and I am certain you look up at times and wonder, "Where did the day go?" Begin today by remembering that God knows exactly what you are able to accomplish. Instead of being preoccupied with your list, just breathe, then ask God what should come first, next, and last. Proceed according to God's ordering of your steps.

Instead of walking through life holding your breath, as if you are posturing for the next blow, take at least five minutes today and every day to get grounded on your floor, and just breathe in the presence of God. Allow the spirit of God to reinvigorate you with new life.

Heavenly Creator, thank you for breathing your very life force into me and for creating me with victory in mind! Order my steps in your word on this day, for you know what is best for me.

Today, I release to God this list of "things to do" in exchange for peace and gratitude:

....

....

....

....

Don't Take Your Tribe for Granted

When you come together, each one has a hymn, a lesson, a revelation, a tongue, or an interpretation. Let all things be done for building up.

~1 CORINTHIANS 14:26

Women have work to do in terms of truly embracing one another. Get a few in the same room, and a silent competitiveness ensues. We've gotten so good at this game of "Who's the queen bee?" that we don't even need words to play it! We've become masterful at innuendos, and the emotional energy we often carry around one another, while concealed, is easily detectable.

Sure, we exchange smiles and casual conversation, but the internal monologue sounds more like, "Wonder where she got those shoes," "Nice lipstick color," "Do I look okay?" or "She's really beautiful." But none of this ever crosses our lips. We carry on, not having offered a compliment nor taken the opportunity to uplift each other. When you notice a woman with a gift, thank her for her talents! God needs as many of us as possible to come together and shine bright in the world.

I grew up with a younger brother whose skin was lighter than mine and who had green eyes. Thankfully, I no longer believe in the "lighter is righter" deception. As a child, however, I felt I didn't receive as much attention from my female family members as he did. For this reason, the story of the ugly duckling growing up to be the beautiful swan really appealed to me. From very early on in my life, I made it a point to genuinely compliment other women, because I never want any woman to feel like I did. I've also discovered that the more beauty you can see in others, the more beauty you will see within yourself. We are all mirror reflections of the things we choose to see.

Your tribe may be filled with all types of women. Don't be put off by the woman who does not smile easily, reach out regularly, or compliment others—she may be suffering from low self-esteem. Rather than take it personally, give her the love she believes she is missing by focusing on her gifts and offering *her* a sincere compliment. Let's all help women collectively heal our wounds by building each other up through acts of true love and unity.

Heavenly Creator, thank you for making me aware that I can help myself and other women understand that true beauty is expressed through love, wisdom, understanding, and humility. Teach me how to be more of all of these things.

Today, I am grateful for the beauty in my humility. I will express it by expressing what I admire about:

....

....

....

....

....

A Light in the Darkness

Light dawns in the darkness for the upright;
he is gracious, merciful, and righteous.

~PSALM 112:4

Did you ever think things couldn't get worse, and then they did? After I'd been divorced for about a year, I found myself living with my mom and struggling to put my life back together. I was a manager for a large banking corporation, yet each day was becoming more and more disengaged from my job, my peers, and my staff. One of my direct reports made a very big mistake, which cost the company several thousand dollars in penalties. I should have caught it, but, because my life was in shambles and I was coming in to work exhausted, I didn't. My direct report was fired, and so was I.

With all this darkness, I desperately yearned for the light. Just weeks prior to getting fired, I had met a wonderful man who is now my amazing husband of 11 years. When I got the courage to break the news to him that I'd been fired on top of everything else I was going through, he told me not to worry and to see it as an extended vacation, then he offered to fly me to lunch. Rather than crawl under a rock and never come out, I decided to take his advice. I think I fell in love with him the day he became my private pilot!

I spent a few weeks reflecting on my life and asking for God's mercy, forgiveness, and grace to help me put my life back together better than ever. With a new attitude, I applied for a few job openings. Within two short months, I was employed again. We all must travel though the darkness on our journey to the light!

No matter what you might be going through, there is no darkness so dark that God's light cannot pierce through. It's a new dawn; it's a new day. Allow God's love, mercy, and grace to shine a new light by laying at his feet any darkness in your life.

Heavenly Creator, I am grateful that I need not hide from the dark places in my life, for you already know the cause of my sadness and pain. Give me the strength to not wallow in the darkness but rather to turn to you for the light that will lead the way.

Today, I am grateful to shine God's light in the darkness by acknowledging the good in these experiences:

....

....

....

....

....

Attracting a Spiritual Man

Blessed is the one who finds wisdom, and the one who gets understanding, for the gain from her is better than gain from silver and her profit better than gold.

~PROVERBS 3:13–14

In my line of work, I encounter countless women who have been scorned by men. I've heard complaints about how men send mixed messages, don't communicate effectively, or are noncommittal. These women are perplexed by how a man could "love" her so well but the moment they disengage, he completely disengages.

I've grown accustomed to witnessing the shock on a woman's face when I tell her that her boyfriend or husband is a reflection of her beliefs. I ask, "What private dialogue do you have with *yourself* about men? Do you effectively communicate with *yourself* your own desires about what is possible for you in love and in life? Are you committed to loving *you*?" Thankfully, the solution is as simple as changing our habits of thought.

All men are calibrated to seek God, simply because they, too, are made in God's image and likeness. When a man finds God in you, he will be willing to do whatever it takes to remain by your side. What attributes of God are men seeking? They are outlined for us in the Bible story where a father instructs his son to seek the *feminine* qualities of wisdom and understanding. Yes! In the book of Proverbs, the Bible refers to wisdom and understanding as *she* and *her* more than 20 times!

Think of a woman who is happily married. You may be surprised to find that her level of outward attractiveness has nothing to do with the love she receives from her husband. A man of God will not approach you unless he perceives in his heart that you are walking in or seeking the power of wisdom and understanding in your own life. When you align yourself with this biblical truth, men will be drawn to you, so be sure to use wisdom when deciding which one to give your attention to! A spiritual man will communicate to you by his words and deeds that it is the most *sacred* wise and loving parts of you that make you truly an attractive force.

Heavenly Creator, allow me to love me first, and thank you for helping me understand it is not my looks that will attract love into my life. It is my ability to walk in the wisdom and understanding of myself and my truths.

Today, I will devote 20 minutes in silence with God to gaining deeper wisdom and understanding about myself in these areas:

....

....

....

....

....

Day 19

The Art of Falling Forward

"Blessed are those whose transgressions are forgiven,
whose sins are covered. Blessed is the one whose sin
the LORD will never count against them."

~ROMANS 4:7–8 NIV

For most of my life, I felt the suffocating heaviness of guilt and shame. I just couldn't figure out why I kept making the same mistakes over and over and over again! Like disciple Paul, I had a thorn in my side (2 Corinthians 12:7). I persisted in doing the thing I did not want to do. Like King David, my lustful sins were ever before me (Psalm 51:3). Many of the regrettable actions I took on my journey to experience true love caused me deep despair. But unlike Adam and Eve, who tried to hide their sins from God, I exposed my sins in humility and truth; and I am grateful that God has forgiven me.

Be it through gluttony, gossip, jealousy, racism, procrastination, lying, or lust, God knew that in this fallen world, we would face much temptation, and many of us would succumb to sin. Thankfully, God provides a way out through the love and forgiveness of Jesus Christ.

Satan, also called the accuser, does not want you to know that. He wants to carry on as an evil prosecutor, looking to win his case against you, with no regard nor sympathy for the ignorance or emotional pain that caused you to sin in the first place. Thankfully we don't serve Satan—we serve God, who not only will forgive you but will never count it against you! Hallelujah! Glory in the highest praise!

Whenever you feel guilt, shame, or self-loathing for your wrongdoings, remember, a saint is just a sinner who fell down and got up! Confess your sins, get back up each time, and allow your fall to propel you forward in your relationship with a God who is not concerned with what you did last summer or that time you left home but only rejoices at your return! Like a parent, God loves you that much—what a thing to be thankful for!

Heavenly Creator, thank you for your awesome mercies, kindness, forgiveness, and grace! I release all guilt and shame for my transgressions to you. Thank you for seeing beyond my sin, into my heart, and exchanging my sin for my salvation!

Today, I am grateful to see the following errors or sins as a falling forward because they have taught me:

....

....

....

....

....

Make God the Center

"I am the vine; you are the branches. Whoever abides in me and I in him, he it is that bears much fruit, for apart from me you can do nothing."

~JOHN 15:5

Though my husband is the love of my life, we struggled in the beginning of our marriage. Many times we thought we weren't going to make it. I was picking up the pieces from the brokenness of my past life; I don't think my husband was aware of the amount of baggage he'd have to carry in our relationship.

I carried such shame that I wondered how could I truly love my husband, and how I could receive his love. I had given him the job—for which he'd never applied—of making me happy. It wasn't until we were on the brink of separating that I decided to take a sharp turn in God's direction. God revealed that my happiness was my responsibility, and I began to seek him for my joy. I refocused my energy on God. I trusted that if my relationship with my husband was intended to survive, it would, and thankfully it did. We now enjoy a thriving relationship in which we understand that we are one in flesh and in spirit and that we can only truly love one another to the degree that we love ourselves.

It is never anyone else's responsibility to make you happy—or unhappy—nor can anything outside of you give you a fulfilling life. Thankfully, all you must do to find true fulfillment is go within and allow God to take up residence in you. When you abide in God, you will bear much fruit! Focus on the living God inside of you, and there is nothing you can't do!

Although you may stumble through trial and error, the time is now for you to practice making God the center through prayer, reading his word, and meditation. Take inventory of your life. What fruit do you bear? Is it bitter or just right? If you want sweeter fruit, all you have to do is take a deeper walk with Jesus!

Heavenly Creator, thank you for being the vine and the branches of my life. I know my path will be illuminated when I make you the center. I know I can do nothing without you, and I am grateful I don't have to!

Today, I am grateful that rather than trying to do these things on my own, I will abide in you, await your prompting, and bear good fruit:

....

....

....

....

....

Day 21

Finding Your Spiritual Family

"Yes, just as you can identify a tree by its fruit,
so you can identify people by their actions."

~MATTHEW 7:20 NLT

If I asked you to name one person with whom you could share your deepest desires and most vulnerable truths, without feeling embarrassed or judged, who would it be? It's nice to know there are people we can rely on, who stand by us through thick and thin. Yet some of our greatest adversaries may come from those closest to us.

The Bible says that with of all the healing Jesus did, he performed the fewest miracles in his own town. Perhaps it was because the people closest to Jesus had known him only as the little wild child, always running toward his muse and getting into things. Perhaps they judged him as "just a man" who chose a career of manual labor as a carpenter. Can you imagine what happened when the time came for Jesus to stand in his calling and declare that he is the son of God? There were plenty of people around him who did not agree with his perspective about his life nor his calling.

When you begin to evolve, grow, and change by walking more closely with God, your circle might also change. How do you discern whether the people in your current circle support or hinder your growth? How do you choose spiritual family—those who will inspire you and bring you to higher heights as opposed to lower lows? Thankfully, it's as easy as knowing a tree by its fruit!

If your desire is to build a business, have a God-centered marriage, or lose weight, it'd serve you well to spend more time with those who have achieved these things in their own lives. As the Scripture tells us, "Just as you can identify a tree by its fruit, you can identify people by their actions." If the people in your circle are not bearing the fruit you want to eat, *don't bite it*! I am not suggesting you end these relationships altogether. You should, however, love and honor yourself enough to decide how much time and emotional energy you invest in them.

Heavenly Creator, thank you for giving me the ingredients for bearing good fruit by building relationships with those who love, support, and encourage me, not just in word but in action. Help me go out of my way to uplift others generously and often, because I know I will attract those who mirror who I am at my core.

Today, I am grateful to acknowledge the good fruit these individuals bear. I will learn from and support them by:

....

....

....

....

....

Day 22

Alone but Not Lonely

For God alone my soul waits in silence;
from him comes my salvation.

~PSALM 62:1

I know how uncomfortable it can feel to be alone. As a child, I grew
up feeling like no one truly "got me." There were a few glimpses of
sunshine, but oftentimes I felt sad, alone, and confused. I began running
from my loneliness from the time I was twelve until I was well into my
thirties! I would do whatever I could do to escape the discomfort I felt
when I was alone. It wasn't until I handed over my life to God that I
learned the value of being alone.

When I got down on my knees, I discovered a God to whom I could
cry and to whom I could run, a God I could converse with, a God who
would help me discern the difference between what is real and what is only
an illusion. When we allow ourselves to be alone, we will find the one true
love we're looking for. This love will show us which relationships serve us,
the true source of our pain, and the pathway toward our spiritual solutions.

Look at the word *alone* and see it differently. See it as being *all-one*.
God knows how long you'll be single, if and when you'll get married, and
even who you'll meet! Rather than wasting your alone time being lonely,
use it as an opportunity to develop a personal relationship with God by
connecting *all* of you with the *One* who created you.

The sooner you can recognize the qualities of God in you, the
sooner you will start to recognize opportunities for love and com-
panionship. Don't be so desperate to rid yourself of your feelings of
loneliness that you give sacred parts of yourself to a man or other
people God did not call to you. When you let your soul wait upon the
Lord, your waiting will never be in vain.

Heavenly Creator, thank you for being my Heavenly Husband, my Rock, and my Salvation. I will take this opportunity to be alone with you, allowing you to show me the standard for the kind of love you have in store for me.

Today, I am grateful to use the gift of this sacred *all-one* time with God in this way:

....

....

....

....

....

Change Your Mind

Do not conform to the pattern of this world, but be transformed by the renewing of your mind. Then you will be able to test and approve what God's will is—his good, pleasing and perfect will.

~ROMANS 12:2 NIV

The mind is a powerful mechanism of human functioning. It constantly renders its opinions, telling us what to do and what not to do, filling us with thoughts about what is possible and what isn't possible and taking us on mental roller-coaster rides through all sorts of "if/then" scenarios. The fact is that 85 percent of what we think about each day never comes true. That said, consider the amount of time and energy you expend thinking about things that will likely *never* happen!

I have certainly been guilty of being trapped in the vortex of my mind. If you are constantly struggling in your head, it is because your mind has been conformed to the patterns of this world. And because Satan attempts and often succeeds as the temporary ruler of this world (1 John 5:19), the patterns are quite negative.

The mind can be likened to a video recorder that simply wants to replay itself. When you were a child, if you witnessed unhealthy relationships, you will likely find yourself in an unhealthy relationship or single and in constant fear that good men are a rare species. Thankfully, the process of deleting old, outdated recordings is easier than you might think.

Changing your life doesn't begin with changing behaviors or even habits. Changing your life begins with the simple act of changing your mind. Whenever your mind wants to run amok and judge you for not getting enough done, or having that addiction, or telling you it's too late for you to accomplish your goals, implore our *ever-present* God, "Help me be in your *perfect will* in this moment." God may direct you to be still, press forward, take a nap, or say no. Thankfully, when you move *your mind* in the direction of God's prompting, your life will naturally follow.

Heavenly Creator, thank you for giving me power over my mind. I am grateful to know that change is a simple shift that happens through the repetitive practice of changing my mind.

Today, I will change my mind about the following things, trusting that God's good and perfect will may be done:

....

....

....

....

....

Release Responsibility

Brothers and sisters, if someone is caught in a sin, you who live by the Spirit should restore that person gently. But watch yourselves, or you also may be tempted.

~GALATIANS 6:1 NIV

Have you ever been so upset with someone that you wanted to let them have it? Your mind conjures up all the reasons they were wrong and you were right. You wonder if they did their transgression on purpose, and that only fuels your anger. Perhaps watching a person you love do things you consider unhealthy or sinful has made you feel sad, helpless, and hopeless.

Showing disappointment in others can be a way for us to deflect our own unresolved issues. If we peel back the layers, we might find that we are addicted to pain, and what we are witnessing in them is a recurring theme in our own lives. We might secretly believe their behaviors are somehow our fault, or they may be reflecting to us the things we do not want to see in ourselves.

Whenever I was tempted to accuse my husband of not giving me enough attention or to express disappointment in my son for not doing life like I wanted him to, I lovingly stated my case or simply gave it to God. Life got much better for me when I realized that the only one I am responsible for saving is myself because all men have free will.

If you perceive that someone is transgressing against you or themselves, do as God instructs us. Try to restore the person *gently*. Simply tell them how you feel. Express your desires, then release the false belief that your peace is their responsibility. Why risk tempting yourself into a state of anger and frustration when you can have the peace of God?

When you can see that life is a class and everyone is your teacher, you know that your assignment is to learn to live by the Spirit. So when you think someone has sinned against you, ask yourself, "What would Jesus do?" You will receive the insight and compassion you need to respond with love and gratitude to the people in your life for the love lessons they teach you.

Heavenly Creator, thank you for making me aware that you are the only one who can give me peace, and I am the only one who can take it away from myself. I am grateful that whenever I feel upset, I can call upon you to help me find my peace and happiness.

Today, I release the following persons from any responsibility to make me happy. I will remain in perfect peace by:

....

....

....

....

....

Day 25
Think about These Things

Finally, brothers and sisters, whatever is true, whatever is noble, whatever is right, whatever is pure, whatever is lovely, whatever is admirable—if anything is excellent or praiseworthy—think about such things.

~PHILIPPIANS 4:8 NIV

You are a powerful architect in the creation of your life. Look around you at your job, your furniture, your child, your body, your friendships, your spouse. Notice that you are the common denominator in it all. If you look around and see things that you like, thank God for your blessings! Conversely, if you see things you do not like, you can use your free will to create again.

When God created the heavens and the earth, it all began with a thought. God thought of things that were pure, lovely, admirable, and good. God spoke the thoughts, and voilà—it was so! Because you are made in God's image, you have the same ability to create using the power of thought. Look again at the condition of your life, and ask yourself, "How did I create this life before me?" Identify thoughts you've been thinking that are not aligned with God's word, and think new thoughts that are excellent and praiseworthy!

If you want a good man, don't spend your thoughts on how many bad men you've known in the past. If you want a clean home, don't spend your thoughts on how much of a mess you made. Instead, hold in your mind how a good man could be showering you with tender loving care. Visualize your home neat and orderly. Thankfully, your mind knows no difference between reality and a thought. God has blessed you with a powerful mind that allows for abstract thinking, planning, and dreaming. The more you think on good things, the more you will appreciate the blessings that already surround you, and the greater the possibility that you will have more good things to be thankful for. When you focus on what is praise-worthy, you will naturally delineate what does and does not help you press forward toward your goals while also maintaining your peace.

Heavenly Creator, thank you for blessing me with a powerful mind! I will use it to create a life filled with love, peace, and joy by thinking on and striving to work toward only that which is lovely and excellent. I will begin my thoughts today with the truth: You love me, and I love you.

Today, I am grateful for the ability to think about these people, places, and things in positive ways:

....

....

....

....

....

There's Power in Pain

But he said to me, "My grace is sufficient for you, for my power is made perfect in weakness." Therefore I will boast all the more gladly of my weaknesses, so that the power of Christ may rest upon me.

~2 CORINTHIANS 12:9

Do you experience times when you are not at your best? Do you struggle with a weakness so embarrassing it feels like a thorn in your side? Trust that God's grace is sufficient for you. God knows that what you are going through is to help you build your spiritual muscle. It may seem more comfortable for you to cover your pain by wearing a fake mask of strength or hiding behind a smile. But how can God help you heal what you do not reveal?

Life begins at the end of your comfort zone. Stop struggling against your weakness. Instead, acknowledge it. Whatever your struggle, it's okay to ask God for help. Only by your invitation will the Holy Spirit turn your pain into your power! I learned to seek and find my true beauty from within and help other women do the same.

Sadness taught me to have empathy for the circumstances of others. It was only when I gave my weakness to God that his power was made perfect. Yet I am not immune to weakness. I often turn to God in humility, asking for strength to carry me through.

In conversation with God this morning, I expressed through tears the heartbreak I feel at times because of the cost of carrying the cross of my life's calling. Yet a second later I felt a rush of gratitude for the lives I have already helped to heal and surrender to the truth. There is an appointed time for everything, and in that moment I felt called to a quiet, peaceful task. As I gathered ingredients to make slow-cooked chili and cornbread, I listened to good worship music and thanked God for all that I have.

Heavenly Creator, I am thankful that I need not hide my weakness from you. I pray for the strength to speak my hidden truths. I have faith that you will help me find the power in my pain.

Today, I am grateful to shine the light of truth on the following weakness and pain for God's transmutation:

....

....

....

....

....

Day 27

The Fallacy of Judgment

"Judge not, that you be not judged. For with the judgment you pronounce you will be judged, and with the measure you use it will be measured to you."

~MATTHEW 7:1–2

Admittedly, the initial read of this Scripture from the book of Matthew instilled in me the fear of God! Haven't we all fallen into judgment before? To know that *you will be judged in the same measure you use to judge others* may be a bit unsettling. Especially because we get our cues about people based on how they dress, what they have, what they say, what they do—it seems almost impossible not to judge, right? Not exactly. There is a difference between judgment and *observation without condemnation.*

As women, we've been collectively conditioned to judge by appearances. We want people to tell us we are pretty. We wanted our dolls to be pretty, our clothes to be pretty; everything had to be made prettier by adding a little more of this and a little more of that, and many of the add-ons were in the form of external things over internal substance. The consequence is that we have unconsciously created a feminine value system in which we endorse "judging a book by its cover." Why, when we do not know the full story?

The fallacy of judgment is that whatever faults we see in another person are the same faults we see *and* solidify *within* ourselves. Judgmental thoughts will cause judgment to come upon us, not because God is anxiously waiting to judge but because our thoughts are like boomerangs. Whatever messages we send out into the universe will be returned to us.

Whenever you are tempted to judge another woman, stop and instead look for the beauty in her—her humility, wisdom, or courage. Seek to discover the strength that God gave her, and gladly tell her what you see. In doing so, you will find more of these God-given qualities within yourself. Life is always more beautiful when we look beyond the surface!

Heavenly Creator, thank you for helping me understand the fallacy of judgment. Teach me to love others by finding their true beauty and seeing them as direct reflections of me and you.

Today, I am grateful to release these judgments about others in exchange for a lovelier version of them and me:

....

....

....

....

....

Day 28

The Armor of God

Put on the whole armor of God, that you may be able to stand against the schemes of the devil.

~EPHESIANS 6:11

I'm sure when you leave the house today, you will have your purse, your shoes, your ID, and your cash, but will you also put on the whole armor of God? As much as we may not want to acknowledge it, there is an enemy who has many names, including the "prince of the power of the air" (Ephesians 2:2). He roams around day and night, through the airways or winds of life, seeking someone to devour.

In my work as a spiritual advisor, I have found that most people get blinded by the schemes of the devil because they do not place all their trust in God's word. They might say they hear the word of God, but the fruit of their lives is a sure sign of their truth. Thankfully, you have the power to cause the devil to flee simply by putting on the armor of God.

The book of Ephesians gives us specific instructions for how to armor up for the big world out there. This involves equipping ourselves with truth, righteousness, readiness, faith, salvation, and prayer. Wow, that's quite a list! But if you stop and think about each of these qualities, it becomes clear that they are all parts of a whole—a state of consciousness that can be achieved by moving through your day with a thoughtful and peaceful attitude.

When you realize that God is everywhere and especially inside you, you can be reassured that you are never alone. You are walking with God, with thought and purpose, through your day, surrounded by and aware of the beautiful signs of God, and protected from the minutiae of petty nonsense. When you begin to feel the armor weakening as your day wears on, stop and say a prayer of gratitude for all he has given you, and ask for continued strength. Stand against the schemes of the devil by wearing the armor of God, and the devil cannot stand a chance against you!

Heavenly Creator, thank you for giving me the ability to withstand the darts of the devil without being pierced by wearing the full armor of God each day. I am grateful to know that when I remain in truth, righteousness, and readiness, I am protected, and no weapon formed against me shall prosper!

Today, I am grateful to strengthen my armor of God by studying this Scripture and journaling what it means for my life:

....

....

....

....

....

Believe in God's Blessings

"The thief comes only to steal and kill and destroy. I came
that they may have life and have it abundantly."

~JOHN 10:10

Have you ever been on the brink of a blessing, yet you couldn't experience the fullness of joy due to the internal dialogue that immediately rushed in to bombard your thoughts? Take a moment to reflect on a time when God answered your prayers. Maybe you wanted the engagement, the baby, the opportunity, the healing. Whatever it may be, we imagine how happy we'll be when we receive it, but when the blessing arrives, we have a hard time experiencing the joy we expected it to bring.

I can think of countless times when this occurred in my life. I was elated when the love of my life finally asked me to marry him! But my mind immediately shifted to the stress of the dress, losing weight for the wedding, and the wedding planning. Our cross-country relocation was granted—what a blessing! But what about the months and months of stress over the credit card debt we incurred to make it all happen?

While Moses did answer God's calling to lead the Israelites on the exodus out of Egypt, many of them did not reach the promised land because they had too quickly forgotten the hardship and pain from which they were being delivered. Instead, they became overwhelmed by the many days without water, and the manna they were given for food became unappetizing quite quickly! Their lack of belief caused not only their worship of false gods but, ultimately, the death of many of them.

The Scriptures tell us that Satan comes only to steal, kill, and destroy. What better way for the enemy to steal what he cannot kill than by causing you not to believe in God's blessings while in the wilderness of your life? The journey to your promised land will get difficult at times, but if you trust in the Lord and run and not faint, you will walk and not be weary. The Lord will renew your strength, shower you with blessings, and give you new life!

Heavenly Creator, thank you for being my strength as I take the bold and courageous journey toward my promised land. Help me remember that you are with me when I grow weary. All I must do is call on you, and you will give me new life!

Today, with thanks and praise, I will acknowledge the water, the manna, and all gifts of God that give me life:

....

....

....

....

....

THOSE WHOM
I LOVE, I REPROVE
AND DISCIPLINE, SO

be zealous

and

repent.

~REVELATION 3:19

Day 30

The Power of Discipline

Have you ever had your mind made up about eating healthy, working out, or spending time with God? Maybe you got off to a great start, but then, just like that—you went back to your previous ways. Discipline is hard work, and hard work can be painful! A muscle must break, burn, and ache before it becomes toned, and this same process is necessary for building your spiritual muscle.

As with any loving parent, God will discipline you. Recall that the word *discipline* is a derivative of the word *disciple*. As a child learns to walk, she will stumble a few times along the way. Whenever you stumble, learn from the fall and get back up again. Trust that God knew the "fall" was a necessary part of your spiritual fitness training!

Heavenly Creator, thank you for being patient with me as I work to become more disciplined. Thank you for holding my hand as I evolve from crawling, to walking, to soaring in every area of my life!

Today, I reflect with gratitude on the spiritual muscle you're building in me as I practice the power of discipline in these areas:

....

....

....

Day 31

Awareness in the Aftermath

After the flood, Noah began to cultivate the ground, and
he planted a vineyard. One day he drank some
wine he had made, and he became drunk
and lay naked inside his tent.

~GENESIS 9:20–21 NLT

Undoubtedly, you have experienced floods in your life. The rains come, and clouds loom overhead. You cry until at last you feel a hint of freedom from the pain that caused the storm inside you. The life you knew has been washed away. You can see that new, abundant life is just ahead of you; still, you can't seem to escape your awareness of all that has transpired thus far.

Can you imagine how Noah felt after carrying out God's mission to build an ark for his family and the animals of every kind? The rest of the world was partying, worshipping false gods, and oblivious to what God had shared with Noah, who would have to disregard the ridicule and rumors about how he'd gone mad as he worked day and night on answering the call upon his life.

Many are called, but few are chosen, because living in the aftermath is hard work! Just like Noah, when the storms clear and the waters recede, you must immediately begin to cultivate the grounds in your life. Your new-found awareness will allow you to see the weeds that need to be dug up and the seeds that need to be planted in order to make the garden of your new life beautiful and pristine. Watch for God's presence, listen for God's word, and be thankful you were born with the capacity to answer the call!

Yes, the labor of love you will embark upon as part of creating your new life will at times be exhausting. Like Noah, you may feel a little crazy and even fall asleep naked and uncovered—a vulnerable place to be. The process may cause you to seek the emotional assistance of wine, herbal remedies, or sleep. Do not judge yourself. Maintain your awareness, and accept God's grace! God knew Noah would need a drink or two after all he'd been through, so God gave him a vineyard to make the best wine ever. God doesn't want you to do it perfectly; he wants you to just do it.

Heavenly Creator, I know receiving the promises you have for my life is not going to be easy. Although it will be a messy process, I will remember the promise you gave Noah—there is a beautiful rainbow on the other side of the flood!

Today, I choose awareness in the aftermath of life's storms. I am grateful to acknowledge the following rainbows:

....

....

....

....

....

Day 32

The Truth Will Set You Free

"And you will know the truth, and
the truth will set you free."

~JOHN 8:32 NLT

Have you ever wanted someone to tell you the truth? You believed it would be possible for you to forgive them or help them out *if they just told you the truth*. What if that's what God is waiting for from you? God wants to set you free, but he needs you to use your free will to ask. In order for you to ask the right questions, you must acknowledge your truth.

For many years, I ran from what I believed were my truths; I held on to lies I told myself because I bought into Satan's delusions. I thought I would never accomplish my goals, could never be good enough or pretty enough, and that I wasn't worthy of true love. Even when love was in the air, I invited it in it with apprehension. I subconsciously believed that God could not love me because of the sins of my past.

It wasn't until King David told God the truth—that he had committed adultery with a married woman named Bathsheba and had her husband killed—that he was able to reconcile his relationship with God. In fact, he was later called a man after God's own heart (Acts 13:22). Sure, he suffered consequences. King David impregnated Bathsheba, but she lost the baby. Without the sin, the baby would not have been a possibility, so the consequence seemed quite plausible.

Telling the truth can be painful and scary. But accepting the truth of our worthiness *no matter what* can make us so brave that we find we are able to accept and live up to the glory that *is* our true nature. When you speak your truth, you will discover that much of your residual pain was caused by your exhausting attempts to hide from yourself. Thankfully you can embrace the truth for the liberating gift it is right now! God wants to walk with you through your fears, heartbreak, and perceived failures, as difficult as it may be. I guarantee, the truth will set you free!

Heavenly Creator, I am thankful that I must only confess my sins and insecurities in spirit and in truth, and you will deliver me, for you already know what has transpired, and you've already prepared a way out. I am grateful that I must only shine the light of truth over the darkness in my life, and you will set me free.

Today, it is with a heart of gratitude that I am set free by telling you the truth about:

....

....

....

....

....

Day 33

When You Doubt It, Pray about It

*Jesus immediately reached out his hand and
took hold of him, saying to him, "O you of
little faith, why did you doubt?"*

~MATTHEW 14:31

As a believer of God, do you sometimes get hard on yourself for doubting things in your life? Do you find yourself constantly questioning whether something is from God or if it's just another distraction? Do you doubt you'll succeed when the test finally comes? Don't be so hard on yourself. An often-told Bible story speaks to how even Jesus's disciple Peter, who followed Jesus day in and day out, still had doubts.

One evening, after Jesus had done the impossible and fed 5,000 people with five loaves of bread and two fish, he told his disciples to get in the boat and go ahead of him as he dismissed the crowds, and he took some time away on the mountaintop to pray. While Jesus was away, the winds on the water blew the boat with the disciples out to sea. Jesus walked on water to catch up with them. When the disciples saw him out in the distance, they became afraid, doubting it was him, instead believing they saw a ghost. Jesus spoke to them, saying, "Take heart; it is I. Do not be afraid."

Peter answered him, "Lord, if it is you, command me to come to you on the water." Jesus said, "Come." Peter proceeded to get out of the boat and began walking on water toward Jesus, but when he saw the winds he began to doubt and started to sink into the water. He cried out to Jesus, "Lord, save me." And Jesus immediately reached out his hand and took hold of him, saying to him, "O you of little faith, why did you doubt?"

Everyone has doubts, and carrying them alone is a burdensome task. Today, don't keep your doubts a secret—share them with Jesus. When you doubt it, pray about it, and Jesus will be sure to stretch out his hand, lighten your load, and lead you to calmer winds and safer shores.

Heavenly Creator, I am thankful that I need not hold on to fear and doubt! I believe your word when you say that all I must do is pray about it and have faith. Thank you for safely guiding me through the areas of concern in my life.

Today, it is with an attitude of gratitude that I release the following doubts to you in prayer:

....

....

....

....

....

Day 34

Focus on the Promise,
Not the Problems

Cast your cares on the LORD and he will sustain you;
he will never let the righteous be shaken.

~PSALM 55:22 NIV

Divorcing from my ex-husband was one of my most difficult life experiences. I'd spent 12 years with him, and we had a son who was just
10 at the time. I was extremely concerned about how this change would
impact my son's childhood. How would I begin again? Where would
I even start? These were among the countless concerns I'd have while
pondering the impending changes that would take place in my life. As
frightening as it was, the truth is that those 12 years had been filled with
more pain than love and more sadness than joy—which was why I had
finally reached that life-changing decision.

Later, I would consider that some people are in our lives for a reason,
some for a season, and others for an eternity. A shift happened in my life
when I began to acknowledge the blessings and lessons that had come
through the seasons of our fractured relationship. With that, I eventually got remarried to a man who seemed to appear out of thin air. The
irony is that I had met this man almost two decades prior, during my
high school years. Today I look with wonder at my relationship with this
amazing husband and father figure to my son. I marvel at our lovely
daughter, who absolutely adores her big brother. I am eternally grateful
to say I have a beautiful family, and I know what it feels like to truly be
in love. To this, from that. How could it be? By the grace of God.

You may be concerned about the future of your relationship or perhaps your health. This is your opportunity to focus not on the problem but on God's promise to never leave nor forsake you. Take a moment to thank God for those promises right now, in the midst of it all! Trust that the trials of today will lead you to greater understanding and wisdom and that this too shall pass. Your only work is to cast your cares upon him and believe in God's word.

Heavenly Creator, thank you for the wisdom, understanding, and growth that can come only through these life experiences. Help me know the reason for this season, and teach me to cast my cares upon you, for I know you will sustain me.

Today, I am grateful to cast these cares upon the Lord, taking no thought but rather allowing God to speak:

....

....

....

....

....

Rethinking Money Matters

"You shall remember the LORD your God, for it is he who gives you power to get wealth, that he may confirm his covenant that he swore to your fathers, as it is this day."

~DEUTERONOMY 8:18

The topic of money can be uncomfortable, especially for Christians. Many children of God have been taught that the love of money is the root of all evil. There is a scriptural account in which Jesus asked a wealthy man to give away all his possessions. And Judas delivered Jesus to be hung on the cross for just 30 pieces of silver.

It's understandable why money can be a difficult topic for those who walk in faith, but let's look at God's instructions about money. It is not money itself that is the root of all evil; it is the *love* of money that is evil. This is why Jesus said, "It is easier for a camel to go through the eye of a needle than for a rich person to enter the kingdom of God." (Mark 10:25). Jesus knew that most men seek money for their own glory. But what if God wants to give you financial freedom for his glory? There are countless examples in the Bible of how God blessed his faithful children with unlimited riches and favor. Isaac was able to plant and harvest a hundred times greater than those around him. Joseph, whose brothers sold him into slavery, became second in command of Egypt and used his wealth to feed his brothers and save his country.

Think differently about money. Renew your understanding about why God wants you to be financially free. Psalm 37:19 proclaims that the righteous will prosper in the midst of famine. Instead of thinking about how you could use more money for you, meditate on how you can use more wealth for God. Then turn your focus away from money entirely and toward discovering more about how God has called you to impact the world. What blessings and abundances do you already have to be thankful for? What do you have that you can share with others? When you align your heart, mind, and soul with God's calling on your life, he will bless you with exactly what you need to bring it to pass!

Heavenly Creator, I release all thoughts of lack to you and thank you for my many blessings. I trust you with the bills and other things that require money and shift my focus to the thing that matters most: my covenant with you.

Today, I am grateful to release myself from the following money matters and shift my focus to what matters most:

....

....

....

....

....

Day 36

Single-Eye Focus

"Your eye is the lamp of your body. When your eye is
healthy, your whole body is full of light, but when it is
bad, your body is full of darkness. Therefore be careful lest
the light in you be darkness."

~LUKE 11:34–35

There has been much controversy over why Jesus referred to just one
single eye when he said the eye is the lamp for your body. What could
Jesus have possibly been referring to? Everyone knows that most people
have two eyes. Or do we in fact have three?

Science confirms that we have a pea-size gland in our brain called the
pineal gland that functions much like an eye—in fact, it's been referred
to as the "mind's eye." It's even been noted that the pineal gland contains
retinal tissue composed of photoreceptors, just as we have in our eyes.

Having this information as your foundation, we'll ask again what
Jesus meant when he instructed us to keep our eye healthy and full of
light, lest our bodies be full of darkness. Let's start with the literal eyes.
Whatever you take into your body enters in through the lamp that is
your eyes. If you focus on good things, you will feel good inside. If you
focus on bad things, you will feel bad inside.

That's where the third eye comes in. It's what you see when your eyes
are closed, from within your *mind's eye*, that will bring you either death
or life, sickness or health, and self-pity or gratefulness. Test your light
by entering every situation with single-eye focus. Do the programs you
watch each day give you greater awareness, peace, and understanding,
or do they cause you to consume gossip, violence, anger, lust, or strife?
Do you follow your dreams with single-eye focus, or does your brain

scatter in different directions, plaguing you with visions of confusion, scarcity, and lack? Keep your eye healthy! Release the bad by focusing on that which is good, and your whole body will be full of light!

Heavenly Creator, thank you for making me aware of how I can keep my focus on you by filling the lamp of my eye with the light of love, peace, and beauty. I ask that you give me discernment over any darkness I have looked upon, that I may deliver it over to you.

Today, it is with gratitude that I increase my God-given light by removing this darkness from my mind's eye and replacing it with elements of light such as:

....

....

....

....

....

Hallelujah Anyway!

Brothers and sisters, we do not want you to be uninformed
about those who sleep in death, so that you do not grieve
like the rest of mankind, who have no hope.

~1 THESSALONIANS 4:13 NIV

My Uncle Bruce was like a father to me. He always complimented me
and encouraged me to believe I could accomplish big things. He suffered
from muscular dystrophy, which caused his health to deteriorate. He
told me one day he would be gone, and it'd be like "poof!" He'd clap his
hands together when he said it.

I was devastated when I received a phone call saying he was in
critical condition in an ICU. I made same-day travel plans to join my
family at the hospital.

At the airport, I purchased a book to keep my mind occupied with
God's word during my flight, entitled *Hallelujah Anyway*. I came across a
passage in which the author referenced a family member who shared the
same first name as my aunt and the same last name as my uncle. I knew
this wasn't a coincidence.

When I arrived at the hospital, I learned it wasn't my uncle's med-
ical diagnosis that had taken his life. He'd been standing at a stoplight,
and a car crash had happened right in front of him. One car knocked
him straight back with excessive force. He was raced to the hospital
but . . . as he would have said, "Poof!"

My uncle, who had been such a uniquely dear and positive force in
my life, was gone. The sadness I felt was real, yet God has instructed us
not to grieve, as those who do not believe grieve. I miss my uncle dearly,
but I do know in my heart that he was ready to return to God in heaven.

I give thanks for the days I was able to be in his presence. Who have you lost in your life? Honor them today by feeling how they would want you to feel and remembering what they would want you to remember. If it makes you smile, they are smiling, too! So, hallelujah anyway—to the joy they brought you then, to the joy they bring you today.

Heavenly Creator, I am grateful that you know the number of our days. I know that my loved one is resting peacefully with you. Help me not grieve like those who lack faith in you but to see death as an opportunity to connect with your omnipresence in life and in death.

Today, it is with love and gratitude that I shout, "Hallelujah anyway!" as I remember good things about the life of:

....

....

....

....

....

The Sky Is Always Blue

"Look up into the sky, and see the clouds
high above you."

~JOB 35:5 NLT

I suffered from depression for a number of years prior to my ultimate awakening. At the time, I lived in Seattle, Washington. The clouds were usually gray, and the rain flowed like the endless teardrops that swelled from within the depths of my soul. Although barely at times, I was able to function in my depression. I did my best to be a good mom to my children and a good wife to my husband.

One day, my four-year-old daughter and I were sitting in the parking lot of a shopping center. We decided to play "I Spy," that game where you describe something you see, without saying what it is, and the other person has to guess.

When it was my turn, I said, "I spy something really huge and gray. It's up high and it reaches as far as the eye can see." My daughter looked at me with the most puzzled look on her face. I thought, *She must be joking, right?* I proceeded to repeat myself: "It's HUGE, it's gray, and you see it up high all the time!" She looked me square in the eyes and said, "But Mom, the sky is always blue." Wow—out of the mouth of babes!

Whenever you feel down, challenge yourself to give thanks that no matter how numerous the clouds, the sky of your spiritual home is *always* blue. Choose not to focus on the darkness; know in your mind's eye that the light is there. Look for the light that is always available to you. See the clouds in your life with the conscious awareness that they are only temporary. Make peace with the winds, for they have come to blow the clouds away. Keep your head to the sky, and allow the Son to shine his light upon you!

Likewise, the Light of the World has the power to dissipate the darkness of pain, disease, and depression if we don't look down on ourselves or our circumstances. No matter what, keep looking up! Invite Jesus into the darkness, the clouds, and the shadows of your life, and implore him to hold your hand and gently guide you.

Heavenly Creator, I am grateful that you have revealed your truth: The sky is always blue. I look to you! Help me see your bright and shining presence in the midst of the gray, water-filled clouds of my life.

Today, I will go with the flow of the winds in my life with peace, love, and gratitude by:

....

....

....

....

....

Ageless Timeless Love

"I am the Alpha and the Omega,
the first and the last, the beginning and the end."

~REVELATION 22:13

Isn't it good to know that you serve an ageless, timeless God? He is the beginning and the end, the Alpha and the Omega, the first and the last, and everything in between. Who, then, are we to be concerned about age when our Creator is a God of the ages? Who are we to worry about time when our God is a timeless God? Just as the universe has no beginning and no end, neither do you. You are made of the same *exact* star stuff as is out in the space-time continuum, only in varying quantities.

It is so easy to get caught up in what we look like. If you're married or in a committed relationship, you might find it strange when your significant other tells you how beautiful you are without makeup. They are simply seeing a truth within you that you might not see. Sometimes our beauty radiates more brightly when we don't cover it up with powder and fluff!

When I turned 40, I accepted the fact that there was nothing I could do to turn back the hands of time. I was going to either embrace aging or spend my days hating myself and resisting the truth: "Charm is deceptive, and beauty is fleeting" (Proverbs 31:30 NIV). I decided to embrace the truth. I am ageless and timeless. The God *in me* is all that God's children really want to see!

Whenever you begin to analyze, criticize, and judge yourself in the mirror, look yourself square in the eyes and say, "I am ageless, timeless love, made in the image and likeness of the Creator of the universe!"

Remind yourself that those who love you fell in love not with your flesh but with your spirit. This is because they can sense, see, and admire the beautiful star you are!

Heavenly Creator, thank you for helping me see the ageless and timeless love you created when you created me. Help me focus not on my flesh but on my spirit, that I may be a glowing reflection of your glory, which shines through all eternity!

Today, with a spirit of gratitude, I release the self-critic by acknowledging and loving these eternally beautiful qualities within me:

....

....

....

....

....

Awaken in the Affliction

*If your law had not been my delight, I would have
perished in my affliction.*

~PSALM 119:92

The workplace can be a pseudo family. You expect the members of the family to get along and have each other's best interests in mind, but how often do you see a family where everyone is in accord? I remember several instances where I felt afflicted in the workplace as a result of interpersonal dynamics. One stands out more than others. The time had come for me to do a 360 review, a process in which you solicit anonymous feedback from colleagues about your performance.

I chose only one manager to assess me. He was new to the organization, and the plan was that I would report to him in the next couple months. I thought having him review me would give me a good sense of how he felt about my performance. When I received my review, it caused me deep pain to read his defaming comments about me. I called him right away to discuss the feedback. He stuttered through our call and didn't provide me with any rationale for his actions. I asked that a representative from our human resources department be present for our next call. He canceled that call and was a no-show for another. After further investigation, HR informed me I would not report to him.

Of course, we still had to work in the same office. I prayed for guidance. Although I had my suspicions as to why he'd disparaged my work, they did not matter. God told me my role was to make peace with the situation and move on. Our interactions in the office were awkward, but I made a point to treat him with kindness and compassion.

I'm sure you can think of a time when engaging with certain people felt like an affliction. Rather than try to figure out what you can do to fight back, choose to *awaken in the affliction* by realizing it's not about you—it's about them. Release your concerns about the judgment of others and continue to cherish yourself while forgiving others in love, as God has forgiven you.

Heavenly Creator, my afflictions are always oppor-tunities to awaken and delight in your laws of love. I know you are the Almighty and nobody else has power over me. I pray for the ability to respond to my afflictions with love, kindness, forgiveness, and truth, for in every affliction is a lesson you would have me learn.

Today, it is with forgiveness and gratitude that I release myself from the following afflictions and focus on your law:

....

....

....

....

....

An Attitude of Gratitude

*And whatever you do, in word or deed, do everything
in the name of the LORD Jesus, giving thanks to
God the Father through him.*

~COLOSSIANS 3:17

One of the best ways to maintain an attitude of gratitude is through
the act of journaling about all you have to be thankful for. When you
do, you are sending a love letter to the universe, acknowledging the
parts of your life that bear witness to God's love. The universe is quick
to respond by giving you more to be grateful for.

When I gave my life over to Christ, I made it a point to guard my
mind by journaling daily. I would gather up my writing instruments,
grab my earbuds, and prepare with excitement to jot down my recol-
lections of all God had done for me. One day, for no apparent reason,
I began journaling about my daughter's little fish, Blue Sky.

Blue Sky had an excited, playful personality. He would perform a
show for us whenever we approached the fish tank. He'd follow our fin-
gers as we gently slid them along the glass. I felt deep joy and gratitude
for this magnificent little creation of God.

When my journaling session was done for the day, I packed up
and proceeded back home. No sooner had I opened the door than my
daughter greeted me with excited urgency. She yelled, "Mom, why'd you
take Blue Sky out of his fish tank?" I gave her a little puzzled, worried
laugh and said, "Now, you know I wouldn't do that." Her response:
"Uh-huh. . . . Daddy is putting him back in the tank right now."

Apparently, just before I returned home, my daughter had walked into her bedroom and found Blue Sky on the floor. He had jumped out of the little hole in the top of his fish tank. I returned just in time to watch as the little blue fish slowly regained his life. Within a few minutes, he began to swim.

I know God has performed a miracle in your life so great that you felt heaven and earth collide. Honor all of the miracles, small and large, by taking today to reflect with an attitude of gratitude.

Heavenly Creator, help me do all things with thanks and praise in the name of Jesus Christ, whose life, death, and resurrection are responsible for the many miracles in my life. I ask that you help me watch my words and my deeds, that I may keep an attitude of gratitude in all things.

Today, it is with an attitude of love, reverence, and gratitude that I remember these miracles in my life:

....

....

....

....

....

Day 42
A Time for Everything

For everything there is a season, and a time for
every matter under heaven.

~ECCLESIASTES 3:1

Ecclesiastes tells us there is a time for everything under the sun. A time to be born, to die, to plant, to uproot, to break down, and to build up. Time is a terrible thing to waste. One of the easiest ways to waste your time is by spending it resisting the present moment. No matter what is being presented in your life right now, do not miss God's signs during this time.

Do you believe God knew you would be right where you are now? Answer with an audible yes or no. Prove to yourself that you not only hear God's word but listen to and follow it. So often, we think that in order to be in God's favor, our lives must be perfect, but God tells us that seasons change. There is a time for every matter under heaven. I'll bet the story of the most inspiring person you can think of involved great loss at one point (or many). The easiest way for you to move through the time you are in is by recognizing the gift in the present moment.

What is the sunshine without the rain? The light without the darkness? Joy without pain? God is in all things. These seeming opposites are not opposites at all; they represent the beautiful balance that happens when things are allowed to be what they are at any given moment under heaven. Here lies your power to delete the illusion of separation and duality from your mind.

We must kick the habit of labeling the seasons in our lives as good or bad. Sometimes things just are what they are, and that's okay! There is a season when you can do yoga, go on vacation, have dinner on the table consistently, and be present with your children, and there is a season when you just simply cannot. For every season, take time to thank God for being with you through it all.

Heavenly Creator, thank you for being present in the midst of my every experience. I release my concerns about what is happening in my life right now. Help me receive with gratitude the gift this season—whatever it may be—is offering me.

Today, I will focus, with an attitude of gratitude for your presence, on these matters that require my attention:

....

....

....

....

....

Dealing with Denial

Peter said to him, "LORD, I am ready to go with you both to prison and to death." Jesus said, "I tell you, Peter, the rooster will not crow this day, until you deny three times that you know me."

~LUKE 22:33–34

One of the most hurtful things a person can do is deny your truth. How was it that Jesus dealt so well with Peter's denial of knowing him at the time of his crucifixion? Peter denied Jesus three times by saying to those claiming he knew Jesus, "I do not know what you are talking about." Notice, Peter did not just flat-out lie by saying something like "I do not know him." Whenever a person denies you, it is often an indication that their pain over the reality of your truth is too heavy for them to carry, so they default to claiming ignorance as if they don't know what you are talking about.

Yes, your coworker could have been more professional, your significant other could have apologized, and your parent could have believed you and supported you. Yet God put these people in our lives. Perhaps beyond the burden of hurt they inflicted, we need them to help us cultivate the transformative gift of forgiveness.

In the same way that Jesus forgave Peter for his temporary insanity, pray this prayer we all know so well: "Forgive them, Father, for they know not what they do." Forgiveness does not always come easily, but when you are able to forgive, you will have no anger, no hate, no frustration, and no feelings of betrayal to hide or deny. More important, you will have no reason to be in denial of the healing power of God!

Heavenly Creator, thank you for helping me forgive those who have claimed ignorance to knowing my truths, including myself. I know forgiveness will bring me peace, and I am grateful to you for that. I commit to dealing with the areas of denial in my life, so the glory of truth may shine through me.

Today, it is with courage and gratitude that I forgive the following people who have denied my truths:

....

....

....

....

....

Day 44

The Power of Prayer

And the Holy Spirit helps us in our weakness. For example, we don't know what God wants us to pray for. But the Holy Spirit prays for us with groanings that cannot be expressed in words.

~ROMANS 8:26 NLT

Prayer is a direct line of communication with God. In order to receive his blessings, you must ask and believe. But what if your heart is so heavy that you do not know what to pray for? Sometimes our longings can be so deep we cannot even find words. Thankfully, the Holy Spirit who lives within you is always on standby, waiting to decode and deliver to God the whispers of your heart.

There were times when I prayed with joy and thanksgiving. There were times when I prayed for forgiveness and understanding. There were times when I cried out in agony, and there were other times when I simply sat in silence. No matter how you pray, God hears it all. It does not matter how many or how few words you use. The only thing the Holy Spirit needs to rush to your aid is your sincerity and surrender.

When Moses pleaded with God that he couldn't speak in front of Pharaoh because of his insecurities about his speaking abilities, God sent Aaron to speak on Moses's behalf, commanding Pharaoh to let the Israelites go. When the woman with the issue of blood simply reached out her hand in faith, she was healed. Countless miracles in the Bible document the power of prayer. Take this day to pray continually. Pray with sincerity and belief. If you are unsure what to pray for, simply say a prayer of thanks. Let God do the rest, with faith that he surely knows exactly what you need.

Heavenly Creator, thank you for the Holy Spirit helper you divinely hardwired within my being when you created me. I ask with sincerity that you hear and respond to the desires of my heart, even when I cannot find the words to express my deepest longings to you.

Today, it is with belief and gratitude that I write a prayer that comes not from me but through me:

....

....

....

....

....

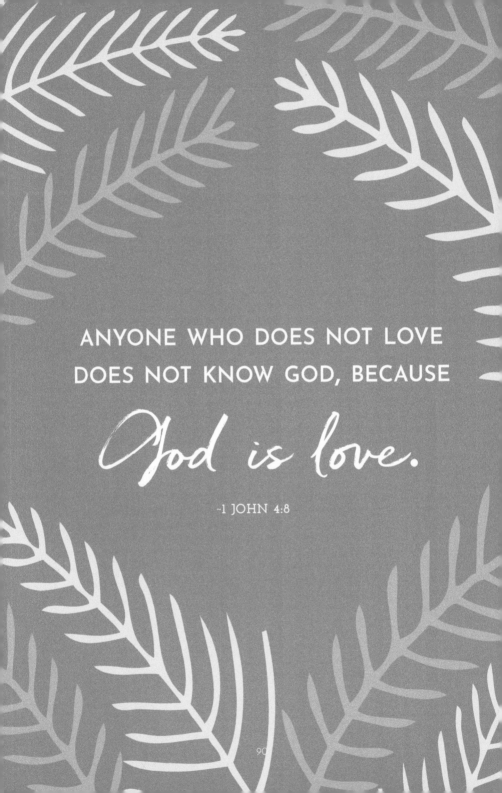

ANYONE WHO DOES NOT LOVE
DOES NOT KNOW GOD, BECAUSE

God is love.

~1 JOHN 4:8

The Truth about Love

Throughout the Bible is this truth: God is love. When you think of love, you might identify feelings for people, places, and things. But when it comes to ourselves, love can seem inapplicable.

The truth is that for you to love God, you must love yourself. You are the vessel, the Body of Christ. If you want to love God more intimately, love yourself more intimately. Start by thinking of one thing you like about yourself. Perhaps your best quality is graciousness, or maybe you always help others. Who do you think is responsible for these wonderful attributes?

Loving yourself has little to do with your clothes, your makeup, or anything outside of you. Only when you recognize all the ways in which the light of God's love flows through you will you be able to shine as brightly as you were made to.

Heavenly Creator, thank you for helping me be more like you by allowing your love to flow through me. I am love! Nothing less will do to describe who you are in me and who I am in you.

Today, it is with deep gratitude and self-love that
I acknowledge all that is lovely and godly about me:

....

....

....

....

Speak Life over Your Life

"For whoever has will be given more, and they will
have an abundance. Whoever does not have, even
what they have will be taken from them."

~MATTHEW 25:29 NIV

When we find ways to be grateful while in the experience, we discover
the blessing in disguise. If we focus instead on what we've lost, we will
find ourselves in various versions of the same situation over time, as like
attracts like. Scripture tells us that to the one who has, more will be given.
For this reason, it is important to find a way to be grateful in all things.

I was once in a minor fender bender. No one was hurt, but my car
was six years old, so the cost of fixing it outweighed its value, and my
insurance company considered it totaled. The problem was that my
husband and I had recently filed for bankruptcy. We made pretty good
money on paper, but what bank would overlook the big red bankruptcy
stamp on our credit reports?

We applied at a car dealership that offered in-house financing to
high-risk customers. I felt good about the process. I thanked God in
advance for a car that would support our family dynamics. But initially
we were denied. I was devastated.

My instinct told me to buy the general manager a card, write a note
expressing my sincere intention to make payments on time, and assure
him we were a risk worth taking. The car dealership overturned their
initial decision, and we were approved to lease a brand-new car. Every
three years, I turned in my leased vehicle for the current year's make and
model. I continued this business relationship for seven years, until the
bankruptcy was absolved.

No matter how bleak it looks, speak life over your life! How else could you possibly experience the gift of gratitude? The finances may be dry, but declare there's just a temporary clog in the funnel. My credit cards may be maxed, but I know these seeds I'm sowing in this other area of my life will reap a harvest! That check bounced, but it only sweetens the story of my trials to triumph and keeps me humble in my victory!

Heavenly Creator, help me actively believe and embody your word. No matter how things appear, help me speak life, because I know that whether my focus is my problems or your promises, "to the one who has, more will be given."

Today, I receive the gift of gratitude by telling God "thank you" for these things in my life:

....

....

....

....

....

Day 47

Choose Love

But God shows his love for us in that while we
were still sinners, Christ died for us.

~ROMANS 5:8

No matter the state of mind you may have woke up in this morning,
fix your thoughts on love and abundance. If God can steadfastly love
humankind while we are in sin, you can still love you! God never said,
"I'll love you if you perform flawlessly and without failing." God sent
us a helper to deliver us out of our troubles.

You are a beautiful, lovely, and amazing *mess* at times. You may often
falter in your faith, but God loves you all the same! Moment by moment,
you have the choice to either live in hopelessness and despair or choose love.
Whenever you choose love, you choose God. I know this sounds easier to do
than it is for many of us. Our minds are exceptionally skilled at giving ourselves compelling reasons to conclude that God's love doesn't apply to us.
We will be tempted to blame ourselves, deny our efforts, and disbelieve that
blessings are intended for us—but don't buy into that program!

God's most powerful messengers have transcended the messiest of
lives. God is patiently waiting for you to do your part in co-creating
your life by loving yourself in the midst of your messiness, so you can
"make your mess your message."

Heavenly Creator, thank you for helping me break free from the "I don't love me" trap! I ask that you help me shine a light on the negative internal dialogue in my mind by relying on you to help me choose love.

Today, I am grateful to expose and heal these things that have prevented me from embracing my love for myself:

....

....

....

....

....

Day 48

Divine Delays

For he says, "In a favorable time I listened to you, and in
a day of salvation I have helped you." Behold, now is the
favorable time; behold, now is the day of salvation.

~2 CORINTHIANS 6:2

Have you ever painstakingly waited on the Lord? You worked hard, you
did what you had to do, yet you were *still* waiting for that breakthrough,
and—nothing. You were certain that you followed God's will. You listened to your heart as you pressed forward in faith through open doors,
closed doors, and all manner of uncertainty. And now you must . . . wait?

When I was waiting, I dealt with negative emotions while holding
tight to my faith and God's grace. I pressed through, knowing that God
didn't bring me this far just to leave me.

When God's promises finally come to pass, you realize how much
time you wasted worrying, complaining, and choosing fear over faith.
Once you're on the other side, it suddenly makes sense why some doors
were opened while others where shut, why you didn't heal right away,
and why certain people in your life had to change. You also realize all the
parts of you that changed along the way. In hindsight, you understand
that if you had been in God's favor a moment sooner, you would not
have been spiritually mature enough to receive the blessings with peace,
joy, and love. It simply wasn't your time.

From this point forward, whether it be a meeting, traffic, a grocery store line, a financial breakthrough, your health, or the deepest desires of your heart, see every delay as a *divine delay*. Be thankful and trust that God already knows the day and time to send you the person, the resources, the idea, the open door, and the *favor* of God's salvation in your life!

Heavenly Creator, thank you for divine delays. While I wait, I ask for the ability to trust that you have heard the desires of my heart. I embrace the fact that my not having it now is no indication that you do not desire it for me. I am grateful that you are my helper. Let your will be done.

Today, with patience and gratitude, I release concerns about when or how these things will happen in my life:

....

....

....

....

....

Day 49

Write the Vision

Then the LORD answered me: "Write the vision, make
it plain on tablets, so he may run who reads it."

~HABAKKUK 2:2

Do you have a vision for your life and your family? Whether you
envision financial freedom, a good health report, a God-centered
relationship, or serving the world in a grand way, God would not have
placed the desire in your heart unless he knew you had the ability to
bring it to pass. Sure, there's work to be done for you to answer God's
call, but he has already ordered your steps; you must only surrender
yourself enough to follow the bread crumbs along the way.

Often we get caught up in the details. "What's it going to look like?"
"Who will support me?" "What must I do in order to have the desires of
my heart?" As the saying goes, the devil's in the details. Leave the details
to God, write the vision, and make it plain! In this *law of attraction* age, so
many people use buzzwords like *manifestation* and *visualization*, but many are
still struggling to obtain the things they believe will bring them peace in life.

While creating a vision board can be a fun and rewarding thing
to do, be sure that service, love, and giving are at the top of the list of
what drives your desires. If you want more wealth, what will you use
it for? Whom will you use it to serve? If you want more time, what
will you do with it? How will you use it productively? If you want true
love in your life, are you ready to hold the vision that healthy, intimate,
God-centered love is possible?

Journal with gratitude regularly, and as you write the vision for your life, be sure that whatever you ask for you are also ready to give, for this is the reciprocity of love; whatever you send out into the universe will surely come back to you. Many of my visions have come to pass, and many have not; still, I am grateful for it all because I trust that in God's timing, he will answer my every call.

Heavenly Creator, thank you for giving me great visions for my life. I know you put the dream in my heart because you created me with the ability to bring it to pass. I release the how, what, when, and where to you and ask that you help me hold the vision, as you already drew it when you created me.

Today, it is with deep gratitude that I visualize, with a smile, these experiences you have in store for me:

....

....

....

....

....

Run with Perseverance

Therefore, since we are surrounded by such a great cloud of witnesses, let us throw off everything that hinders and the sin that so easily entangles. And let us run with perseverance the race marked out for us.

~HEBREWS 12:1 NIV

Do you remember being in a race as a child? You start off strong, with a huge, playful smile on your face as you jet off in glee, with high hopes you'll win the race, but about halfway in, you start to tire. You no longer have that perfect runner's posture, nor is your face graced with that big, confident smile. You sloppily flail your way to the finish line, tired and worn, but, hey—you made it!

This is much like the journey you will take when you decide to answer God's calling in your life. God might be calling you to start a new endeavor, persevere through a challenge, act on a long-held desire, or simply remember him throughout the course of your day. Even when we feel certain of what our next step should be, we can be hesitant to undertake it—for fear of the unknown, fear of failure, and even fear of success. Our own doubts, not to mention the questioning of naysayers in our lives, threaten to stop us before we even start.

God knows your sleepless nights, doubts, emotions, and fears as well as he knows the hopes of your heart. Just as he did with Jesus at the Last Supper, God is preparing a table for you, sometimes in the very presence of your enemies. Keep running the race, knowing that God will give you strength! Move forward by throwing off everything that hinders you, focusing on the path ahead of you, and running the race marked out for you with perseverance. Be thankful, because God is indeed at your side!

Heavenly Creator, I am grateful to know that you are aware of my fears, my doubts, my fatigue, and yet you are still my number one fan, rooting for me! Help me realize that it doesn't have to be pretty; it just has to be. Thank you for giving me the stamina necessary to run the race marked out for me with perseverance!

Today, it is with faith and gratitude that I run the race marked out for me by releasing thoughts that hinder me:

....

....

....

....

....

Day 51

You Are Forgiven!

*If we confess our sins, he is faithful and just to forgive us
our sins and to cleanse us from all unrighteousness.*

~1 JOHN 1:9

As women, we often carry emotional weight with us every day. God said
that if we just confess our sins, we will be forgiven for all unrighteousness.
Whether you've had an abortion, been through divorce, overspent and
caused yourself financial woes, or committed any "sin" you keep beating
yourself up about, today you will stop it! God already knows what you
did and what you're going through. More important, God already knows
why. God knew that the root cause for my sin was that I had unhealed
emotional wounds within me, and until I could resolve them, the
unhappy child inside me would rise up and throw the occasional temper
tantrum. We know now that we don't get what we want by jumping up
and down and screaming—we get what we want by *asking*.

Ask God to forgive you for the sins you think you have committed, and just like that, you are forgiven. To the woman caught in
adultery, Jesus said, "Go and sin no more." To the woman at the
well who had been married five times and was living with her boyfriend, Jesus said, "Go and tell your people about me." Jesus knew
their hearts and gave them the love that covers a multitude of sins.
Today is the day you stop burdening yourself. *You are forgiven.*

Heavenly Creator, thank you for forgiving me for my sins. Thank you for knowing that my heart's deepest desire is to serve you. Help me believe that I am forgiven for even the most egregious of my sins, because you are the loving God I serve.

Today, it is with faith and gratitude that I lay the following sins at your feet. I am washed clean:

....

....

....

....

....

Day 52
Do It for God

*Whatever you do, work heartily, as for the LORD
and not for men, knowing that from the LORD
you will receive the inheritance as your reward.
You are serving the LORD Christ.*

~COLOSSIANS 3:23–24

What if you did everything as if you were doing it for the Lord? How would you get up and start your day? How would you get dressed? What would you wear? How much effort and energy would you put into the task at hand? Ask yourself, how would I do things a little differently if I did them for God and not men (or other women for that matter)?

I once suffered with the need to please men. I'd get dressed wondering if I was pretty enough to be seen or approved of, and my sense of self-worth easily rose and fell depending on how much recognition I received or did not receive. I recall getting my hair braided for the first time as an adult. Initially I experienced anxiety and was afraid to leave the house. I was so preoccupied with concern about whether the world around me would approve of my "new look."

On another very different occasion, I remember going on and on and on to my employer at the time about how qualified I was to take on the additional leadership responsibilities they had approached me about. I remember the director saying, "You don't have to prove how smart you are. We would not have approached you if we didn't believe you could do it." I recognized some uncomfortable truths during moments like these. I wanted the approval of men because I didn't approve of me.

God wants you to turn away from seeking outside validation. You are already approved. As you start your day and show up in the world, do it for the Lord, knowing full well that your rewards and your inheritance lie not in someone else's approval, opinions, or judgments of you. Your rewards come by way of serving Jesus Christ—and be assured, he loves you!

Heavenly Creator, thank you for releasing me from the bondage of concerns about what "man" may think about me. I am grateful that you think I am beautifully, wonderfully, and powerfully made! May I show up in the world with an intention to reflect your divine light from the inside out while also looking for only your light in others.

Today, it is with deep gratitude that I release my ego by letting go of the following things that others might think:

....

....

....

....

....

Speak Life-Giving Words

*In the beginning was the Word, and the Word
was with God, and the Word was God.*

~JOHN 1:1

God said, "Let there be light," and there was indeed light. God said,
"Let us make humankind in my own image and likeness," and we were
created. Words are so powerful that they played a starring role in all of
God's creations here on earth. This is also why the Bible says, "Death
and life are in the power of the tongue, and those who love it will eat its
fruits" (Proverbs 18:21).

Do you know a person who has a habit of using their words in negative
ways? Perhaps they constantly complain about what's going on in their
lives, and as you listen, you can't help but notice that their lived experience
is a reflection of their perceptions. You know that girlfriend who declares
that all men are nothing but horrible liars and cheaters, with no real compassion? What kind of man does she have in her life, if any at all?

As the late poet Maya Angelou said, "Words are things"—indeed, very
powerful things. They affect your brain, your interactions with others, and
your environment. Your words send an unseen, energetic "ask" to God,
and good or bad, our gracious God tends to deliver what we ask for! So no
matter how bleak your situation appears, activate your faith by speaking
life-giving words that will pick you up as well as all those who come into
your orbit. Rest assured, when you speak goodness, you will start to see the
goodness that lies—sometimes hidden—all around you.

Heavenly Creator, thank you for giving me the ability to choose my words wisely. As difficult as my experience may seem, I am grateful that you fill me with hope and resolve when I have the faith to speak words of love and light into my life.

Today, I am grateful to regularly speak these life-giving words of hope, faith, and love over my daily life:

....

....

....

....

....

Day 54

Surrendering in Sickness

*"Fear not, for I am with you; be not dismayed, for
I am your God; I will strengthen you, I will help you,
I will uphold you with my righteous right hand."*

~ISAIAH 41:10

Once, the fear of sickness swept over me like a brush fire. Life was going great, then bam! I discovered a painful knot underneath my armpit. Time for my first mammogram. It was unsettling to enter a room with a large scanning machine, its function to look for something suspicious. I was on pins and needles while awaiting my results.

A week later, I was called back into the office because the doctors found calcium deposits in one of my breasts and wanted to take a closer look. My mind raced as I wondered who would take care of my children and my husband. All sorts of frightening scenarios swirled around in my head. I needed to do something to guard my mind. Even though I was unsettled by fear and despair, I thanked God in advance for my healing.

I knew I had too much work left to do on earth. I decided I would not be dismayed. I recited daily, "I am healed, I am healthy, I am whole!" I journaled regularly and even wrote a future-dated entry for the day of my expected results. The journal read, "Thank you, God. I am eternally grateful to have received the letter in the mail that states I am healthy and free of disease!" As faith would have it, my letter did arrive. The calcified tissue was benign, and my discomfort was perhaps just a reaction to my new brand of deodorant.

Are you suffering with sickness, emotional disease, or even the thought of it? This can be a scary and lonely place to be. Although there may be people sending you prayers and showing you love, you might still be overwhelmed by the negative thoughts in your own head. God says, "Fear not, for I am with you. I will help you; I will strengthen you." Whether you are dealing with a mental health concern, a flu, or even a life-threatening health scare, thank God for his promise to uphold you in his righteous hand!

Heavenly Creator, I am grateful that you are with me, even now, in the midst of my uncertainties. I will not fear; I will not be dismayed. Instead, I will use this time in peace, stillness, and quiet reflection as I take refuge in you to carry me through.

Today, I am grateful to surrender thoughts of fear and anxiety in exchange for this godly perspective, which strengthens me:

....

....

....

....

....

Day 55

Live Like a Child

And said, "Truly, I say to you, unless you turn
and become like children, you will never
enter the kingdom of heaven."

~MATTHEW 18:3

This Scripture quotes Jesus as saying, "Unless you become like children, you will never enter the kingdom of heaven," which may sound like a tall order. Adults generally carry much more weight on our shoulders than children do. There are bills to pay, places to be, people to see, and real day-to-day problems to deal with. Looking at it this way, it would seem impossible to follow this instruction. But Jesus was talking about a state of being.

We know that young children marvel at life. They tend to get very excited about simple things like running through the grass, playing with friends, gazing up at airplanes, or creating their next cool invention! Whatever they are into, they are usually completely enthralled with a sense of wonder and, often, joy. Sure, they get sad, but with a little tender loving care, they are quick to forgive and tend to bounce right back.

Think back to a time when you watched a child creating something from scratch. Can you see that little person working with focus, presence, intention, joy, and confidence? You will generally not find a young child endlessly questioning whether they used the right color, or wondering what someone else is going to think, or stressing over whether they should have picked a different design altogether. Children naturally exhibit their keen ability to experience the kingdom of heaven in our midst.

Whenever you are doing what you do in life, aim to do it with the presence and wonder of a child. Don't question whether you chose the right color lipstick after you already put it on; don't regret the comments you made in the office meeting or become so consumed with what others might think that you do not express yourself at all. This world is your playground. Like children, be present in all that you do, and you will inevitably experience all the simple joys God has for you!

Heavenly Creator, thank you for helping me uncomplicate my life by allowing me to see life through the loving lenses of a child. Help me create like nobody's watching, and help me see perceived obstacles as opportunities for learning and exploration!

Today, with gratitude and a childlike soul, I will begin this new project or activity, experiencing love as it unfolds:

....

....

....

....

....

Day 56

Get Fit with Godliness

*For physical training is of some value, but godliness
has value for all things, holding promise for both the
present life and the life to come.*
~1 TIMOTHY 4:8 NIV

As work and family life takes hold, many of us struggle to prioritize exercise, and we chastise ourselves for our more sedentary lives. Staying in shape was always important to me, but the frequency of my workouts would ebb and flow.

I remember a time when I was preparing for my organization's annual women's retreat, and exercise fell by the wayside. The planning phase was stressful, and I dealt with it by indulging in a few more late-night snacks than usual. I didn't feel good about my body. I thought about starting a vigorous workout routine using a video program called "Insanity." With all I had going on in my life, the thought of adding working out into the mix was in fact *insane*. Then I heard the still small voice within me say, "Just do my will; all areas of your life will be in order."

I went about doing the things God called me to do, which included writing my first book. I found myself so fueled by the desire to write that my late-night snacking tendencies disappeared. When I ate, I kept things simple by eating small portions of healthy, quick-cooking foods. By the time my retreat came, I was full of energy and my body felt strong. I asked myself, would I have felt as good if I had allowed myself to try to work out every day, write a book, cook dinner every night, and plan a retreat? I'm certain the stress hormones would have traveled right from my brain to my gut, no matter how much I exercised.

You are spirit before you are flesh. Believe God's word when he says while exercise is of value, it is not the diet nor the workout that gives you true health and life. It is the spiritual food you receive when you seek godliness that will benefit you in this life and the next!

Heavenly Creator, thank you for helping me see that while physical training is of value, true health and beauty come by way of putting you first. Whether I am in a season of working out or a season of working within, I will go with the flow of the tides and the winds.

Today, it is with an attitude of gratitude that I approach my health in these spiritually grounded, life-giving ways:

....

....

....

....

....

....

Ride the Waves

He made the storm be still, and the waves of the sea were hushed. Then they were glad that the waters were quiet, and he brought them to their desired haven.

~PSALM 107:29–30

In any given season, you may experience the feeling of riding a wave of good fortune. You might also experience being tossed to and fro by the crashing waves in your life. Many times we risk drowning, not because we cannot get through the situation at hand but because we do not trust that this raging water is the path to our promised land. Be still. Be quiet. Grab the life raft of Jesus through prayer, and dive into the living waters of God's word.

I lost custody of my son for a while due to a nasty divorce. After the divorce, I worked hard to reengineer my life so I could offer my son a stable and supportive home with me. In time, I remarried. My husband and I had a daughter together and were raising her in a beautiful house. The only thing missing was my son. I fought seemingly constantly with his father about how he should release control of our son, yet we never got anywhere.

While in prayer, I realized just how exhausting this continual conflict was for everyone, particularly our son. I surrendered fully to the fact that this situation was a consequence of my own actions. I conceded to parent my son from the sidelines, and that's when something happened. My son's father was caught on camera inappropriately roughing him up. The video was reported to me, and I took it to the courts. As a result, I was awarded primary custody of our son. Today, my son and I have a very deep and loving relationship.

Life is full of waves. Turmoil happens. Change happens. Some waves have us riding high; others are unexpected and unwelcome. But when we decide to ride the waves in our life without resistance, the waters will be less choppy. Thankfully, when you receive the love lesson that the storm came to teach you, God will calm the storm and quiet the waters.

Heavenly Creator, thank you for your presence in the midst of the storm. Show me how to float along the unsettled waters in my life so that I may learn the lessons the waves have come to teach me on the journey to my promised land.

Today, I choose to swim in a sea of gratitude by trusting God in the midst of these storms:

....

....

....

....

....

Day 58

Pay Attention Inward Now

*"And I will ask the Father, and he will give you another
Helper, to be with you forever, even the Spirit of truth,
whom the world cannot receive, because it neither
sees him nor knows him. You know him, for
he dwells with you and will be in you."*

~JOHN 14:16–17

If we are God's temples and God dwells within us, why is it that we spend so much time running from ourselves? We look to the world for love, attention, happiness, and even *permission* to do the things we want to do! We are usually left disappointed because people cannot give us what is *our responsibility* to give ourselves. So why don't we go within, to access the greatest love of all, the Holy Spirit?

Throughout my life, I battled with the habitual temptation of running from myself. Even while walking through the doors to my victory, I struggled with the fear of answering my calling. What is it on the inside that we are afraid of? I decided to take the advice of a spiritual teacher and see my resistance and pain as an opportunity to **P**ay **A**ttention **I**nward **N**ow. When I went within to consult with the Spirit of God, the truth became clear.

Going within would require me to clean house! I'd have to acknowledge that I still suffered from the fear of failure. I'd have to admit that I still believed I wasn't good enough. I'd have to accept that my evolving might change the dynamics of my relationships with certain friends and family members. I'd have to embrace the idea that to whom much is given, much is required. Was I ready? I'd be on the hook for doing what seemed so impossible—I'd have to say yes to walking in my God-given divinity.

I never would have known any of my truths had I given up at the first pangs of emotional pain. Allow pain to serve as an internal guide, calling you to Pay Attention Inward Now. Let pain bring you to your knees, to silence, to listening to what the Spirit within is asking of you. You will emerge from your spiritual submersion invigorated, confident, loving yourself, and ready to take on the world!

Heavenly Creator, thank you for helping me honor you by honoring the treasures within me. Help me stand firm in the fact that I do not need the world's approval. I commit to finding the power in my pain by going within rather than outside myself.

I will take my pain to the Holy Spirit within and wait with patience and faith for the guidance in these areas:

....

....

....

....

....

Day 59

Pray without Ceasing

Rejoice always, pray without ceasing.

~1 THESSALONIANS 5:16–17

What is meant by praying *without ceasing*? Praying before breakfast, lunch, and dinner is hard enough as it is! I don't know about you, but sometimes I am so hungry by the time my dinner is made that all I can think about is digging in. Truth be told, I probably enjoyed a nice mini meal while cooking. When my dinner hits the table, I might find myself rushing through the prayer to get to the food.

When I asked God in prayer how I might pray without ceasing, I received the understanding that prayer is not always a ritualistic and organized pause in the midst of activity. Prayer is more about *how* we do the things we do throughout every moment of every day. God wants us to live our lives in a *state of prayer.*

I decided that whenever I cooked, I would cook in a state of gratitude for the nourishment, fragrant smells, colors, and tastes my food provides. Wouldn't you know, my food started to taste better! Whenever I cleaned, I would thank God for the home I was fortunate enough to be cleaning. When I interacted with other people, I would attentively listen to their words and look in their eyes, all the while remembering that they were a reflection of God and treat them accordingly. I decided that my entire life would be a walking prayer.

Prayer is the acknowledgment and active awareness of God's presence in all things, from doing your hair to driving your car to guarding your mind. Thankfully, when you bring God into everything you do, you can't help but rejoice at all times!

*Heavenly Creator, thank you for helping me under-
stand that prayer doesn't have to be perfect; it
doesn't always have to happen in a certain moment
or at a certain time. Help me make my life a walking
prayer, that I may be in your presence at all times.*

**Today, I am grateful to walk in a posture of prayer
during these moments, interactions, and encounters:**

....

....

....

....

....

The LORD

IS CLOSE TO ALL WHO
CALL ON HIM,
YES, TO ALL WHO
CALL ON HIM IN

truth.

~PSALM 145:18 NLT

Day 60

Be True

One thing I believe we can all agree on is that we all have a longing for relationships rooted in love and truth. We want to surround ourselves with people we can trust, and we want to trust we're on the road God has chosen for us. We want so badly for others to do right by us, but the more important question is, "Are you being true to you?"

Do you believe that you are worthy of Christ's gift to humanity? Do you trust that you can heal from the hurt you've endured? Have you taken it all to God in spirit and in truth? Do you live your life with the faith that the kingdom of heaven will be yours? The essence of your true self is the limitless power of God. Move through each day giving glory to God by honoring him in yourself. The truth will set you free!

Heavenly Creator, thank you for inviting me to draw nearer to you by telling the truth. I trust that you already know my deepest, darkest secrets. There is nothing to hide, so nothing can be hidden. Help me draw more closely to you by telling the truth.

I am grateful to shine the light of truth for God to heal these things once hidden within me:

....

....

....

Day 61

I Shall Not Want

The LORD is my shepherd; I shall not want.

~PSALM 23:1

So much of our worry, stress, and disease in life comes from our earthly longings to have financial gains, find love, pursue our passions, and live out our dreams. It can be a very frustrating and unsettling feeling to want something yet wonder if it is in the plan that God had set for your life. How on earth can we move forward in gratitude and praise when longing plagues our hearts?

There's a gospel song I love that says, "After you've done all you can, you just stand!" Stand on the truth that you are the sheep, and the Lord is your shepherd. Stand on the fact that just like the sheep, you do not know where to go. Stand in faith that your shepherd is guiding you, even when you can't see it. Thy will be done!

If only for today, let go of want. Carrying the emotional energy of "I want" carries the same negative vibration as "I don't have." What message do you think wanting sends out into the universe but more want? By turning your words around day by day, slowly you will find that you have turned your life around. Thank God in advance for giving you what he knows is best for you, be they the desires of your heart or something else entirely. Doesn't "Thank you for blessing me with what you know I need" feel a whole lot better than remaining in the desperate state of want? No, you shall not want! Your shepherd is all you need.

*Heavenly Creator, thank you for giving me the clear
vision to see my blessings. I know that I have you,
therefore I will want for nothing. I am grateful to
know that you are my shepherd, guiding me through
the wilderness in the direction of my destiny.*

**Today, I am grateful to release want from my mind;
instead I will thank God for these blessings he has
given me:**

....

....

....

....

....

Thy Will Be Done

*"I desire to do your will, my God;
your law is within my heart."*

~PSALM 40:8 NIV

You know logically that doing God's will can only result in the best possible outcomes in your spiritual growth. With this in mind, you try to start each day with good intentions. Your goal is to be loving, patient, kind, honest, and open to whatever comes your way. Yet it's all too easy for others to throw off our balance with an unkind word or act.

While God's law is within our hearts, too many of us live in our heads. When you agree to walk with God, you are agreeing to walk along the narrow road. Being on the path less traveled means you won't find a lot of people or heavy traffic, and that can cause you to feel loneliness and uncertainty. Sometimes doing God's will may force you to walk away from relationships that do not serve you. This may even include your closest friends and family members.

Making the shift to do God's will is always hard at first. The people around you will likely not be comfortable with how you're no longer game for gossiping or perhaps less readily available for nights out. Thankfully their comfort is not your priority. Your priority is to do God's will by following the promptings of God within your heart so that you can activate his desires in your life.

Heavenly Creator, thank you for placing your laws of love within my heart. As difficult as it may be, I ask that you help me resist the will of man and follow the will of God. I trust that when I put you first, your love and guidance will direct my path toward your purpose for my life.

Today, it is with a heart of gratitude that I make these decisions according to your will:

....

....

....

....

....

Answer the Call!

"For many are called, but few are chosen."

~MATTHEW 22:14

Has God been calling you to do something? Perhaps you've tried to answer the call a million times! You've had some successes, yet maybe the struggles loom most prominently in your mind. Like me, you may sometimes choose to hang it all up. Like me, you may also choose to answer the call again.

I believe few are chosen because few answer. Many of us are so busy listening to the noise around us that we never hear the call from God. I've been there; even worse, sometimes I've wanted to turn away from the opportunity presented to me. At the first sign of adversity, my ego would get offended, and I'd find it easier to put God on hold than move forward through the challenge.

In my career, I knew God was working through me, but my mind would tell me that I wasn't doing as much as I could to help others. I wanted so very much to change lives. The impact of my efforts didn't happen as quickly as I'd expected, and I was very disappointed that the people in my circle stood by as I struggled, failing to provide me with the support I'd believed I could count on. I was often tempted to give up, and sometimes I sabotaged my own progress toward my destiny. Then God reminded me to shift my focus away from my adversaries and onto my advocates. This is mentally a much healthier and more grateful place to be.

Reflect regularly on the people who would not be doing as well as they are today without having been impacted by your love. These are the ones for whom you press forward! Remember the joy in their eyes and the smiles on the faces of those who are blessed because you had the courage to answer God's call.

Today, shut out all the noise, specifically the noise in your mind. Disconnect from social media. Turn off your phone. Do whatever you have to do to stop the ringing in your ears so you may hear the one call that matters most to your life and the lives of those you love. *Answer the call.*

Heavenly Creator, thank you for giving me the ability to shut out the noise around me that I might hear and answer your call today and each day. Help me remember the joyous, peaceful energy I connect with when I dial your number and converse with you.

Today, with faith, peace, love, and gratitude, I will answer God's call by engaging in the following:

....

....

....

....

....

The Way to Love

Love is patient, love is kind. It does not envy,
it does not boast, it is not proud.

~1 CORINTHIANS 13:4 NIV

Love is a hot topic! Singers sing about it. Writers write about it. Preachers preach about it. We all want it, yet too few of us are able to hold on to it. I once believed that being desired by a man was more important than being treated well. Through much heartache and self-inflicted pain, I realized that I had a God-shaped hole, and no man could fill it.

Maybe you think the way to love is in your next pair of shoes, your new hairdo, or the "Likes" you received on your last social media post. Maybe like me, you believe you'll find love when that great guy comes along and tells you how lovely you are. The truth of the matter is that love cannot be summed up as an emotion, nor can it be found in things. Love is a set of core qualities and characteristics that thankfully have been written for us in the book of life. We will attract these core values in others when we learn to embody them within ourselves.

Love is patient and kind. Love does not envy or boast. We tend to show our kindness to others, giving them the benefit of the doubt and overlooking their mistakes, but do you love yourself enough to be patient and kind to *you*? Do you love yourself enough not to envy or covet someone else's life? Self-love turns envy into admiration, boasting into humility, and anxiety into patience and peace. The way to love is through loving God by truly loving you!

Heavenly Creator, thank you for showing me the way to love. I know that as I embody the core qualities and characteristics of love within myself, all that is love will find me by way of people, places, and things. Thank you for being patient with me, as love would be, while I learn to love myself more fully.

Today, with patience, kindness and gratitude, I will follow the way to love by embodying these core qualities within myself:

....

....

....

....

....

Day 65

A River Flowing

"Whoever believes in me, as the Scripture has said,
'Out of his heart will flow rivers of living water.'"

~JOHN 7:38

I remember sitting along a grassy lakefront field, watching the ripples of the water flow gently with the push of the soft breeze. The birds stood in stillness, peacefully taking in the life all around them. There was a large crane that seemed to be keeping me company while she watched her young swim along the shallow water's edge. Interestingly, I felt the calming and centering presence of God whenever I would fix my attention on that mother bird.

I was grateful for that feeling of being one with all of nature, especially considering that moments prior I had almost lost the battle with my mind, which was telling me how I didn't belong on that lake, spending my day in stillness, but that I should show up like other people wanted me to. I should comment more on my friends' social media feeds, or go to that event I had been invited to, or go home and do this or that. As I sat there taking in the beauty all around me, my mind left behind the nagging thoughts.

Off in the distance, I noticed the cars on the main road and the billboard advertisements for the nearby retail stores. I conscientiously took note of the differences between the way man flows and the way nature flows. I felt as though God was saying, "Accept yourself as I have created you, not as man might pressure you to be. . . . Be like a river flowing."

God created our hearts not to desire the hustle and bustle of the shopping malls nor to be among the crowds of cars hurrying from here to there. By your very nature, you function most optimally when your heart, mind, body, and soul are all in flow with the living waters of God's word, which, *if only you believe*, will give you *true life*!

Heavenly Creator, thank you for making me aware that slowing down, not speeding up, will align me with your purpose for my life. I am grateful that you have chosen things in nature to teach me how to be. Help me learn to be like a river, ever flowing toward all you have in store for me.

Today, I am grateful to be a river flowing. In order to grow, I will let go and let these things flow:

....

....

....

....

....

....

Shine Your Light

"You are the light of the world. A city set on a hill cannot be hidden. Nor do people light a lamp and put it under a basket, but on a stand, and it gives light to all in the house. In the same way, let your light shine before others, so that they may see your good works and give glory to your Father who is in heaven."

~MATTHEW 5:14–16

When I decided to draw nearer to God, I began to behave very differently from how my family expected me to. In my family, there were deep roots of vanity and dissension. The love we had for one another was often overshadowed by competition and other unhealed wounds. In many ways, I was right there with them, a by-product of my environment. You can imagine how awkward it was for everyone when I decided to deal with my darkness and turn on the lights!

After I had evolved, I created a spiritual advising organization through which I helped others do the same. I used to wonder why many of my family members weren't eager to learn more about what I had done to set myself free. Eventually I came to terms with the fact that sometimes, when you set your light on a lampstand, you shine so brightly you expose the darkness within others that they do not want you to see. It's amazing how many people run from the light!

Shine your light bright anyway! Be not concerned about the darkness or discomfort others might feel because you choose to be more like God. With regard to my family members, some came around, and for the ones who did not, I do not take it personally. Whenever you can sense that your light might be making another person uncomfortable, know that they are not resisting you. They are resisting the light within you; they are resisting God. But God's light cannot be hidden! Continue to *do you* with confidence, love, forgiveness, and grace! Always remember to pray for those who persecute you, and bless them as you go.

Heavenly Creator, thank you for making me a light in the earth. I am grateful to shine your light, even in the darkness, for I know you have called me to be the light in the earth. I will set my lamp on a lampstand so as to serve as your lighthouse, shining my light for those seeking to become free.

Today, I am grateful to shine my light bright by engaging in the following interactions with confidence, truth, and love:

....

....

....

....

....

Day 67

Overcoming Temptation

No temptation has overtaken you except what is common
to mankind. And God is faithful; he will not let you
be tempted beyond what you can bear. But when
you are tempted, he will also provide a way out
so that you can endure it.

~1 CORINTHIANS 10:13 NIV

Although we were all created with the Spirit of God within us, we are still born of the flesh and can be easily tempted. I'm sure there have been times when you've gotten angry or upset, lost your temper, or called the guy you said you'd never call again. You might be tormented by even deeper temptations—to abuse drugs, smoke cigarettes, or engage in conversation or sexual activity with someone you know will lead you only to pain.

Temptation is a tangible sign that we have become addicted to something that we hope will fulfill a deep need. We may know in our hearts that our greatest needs can only be fulfilled by God, yet we find ourselves running and hiding from him. Oftentimes this is because we fear it's too difficult to change our ways so we may connect with the truth of who we are.

In order to overcome temptation, it's necessary to face the things you're running from head-on. If you are afraid to be sad about a deeply hidden wound, instead of trying to ignore it, allow yourself to face the sadness and cry about it. Talk about it. Scream about it. Jump up and down about it! Move the stagnant energy from your being with purposeful intention. Better to cry a river than to risk having your life completely backed up by the dam. Overcome temptation by agreeing that God is faithful and will not allow you to be tempted beyond what you can handle. Take the escape God always offers you. Sometimes it's as simple as opening the reservoir of your tears and allowing them to flow. Trust that you can endure it! God has the power to bring you though it.

Heavenly Creator, thank you for focusing not on the things I have done when I have fallen into temptation but on providing my escape. I am grateful that your only concern is that I heal the hidden places I've been running from. Give me the strength to face the pain I've been trying to hide, that I may be truly set free.

Today, I am grateful to overcome temptation by no longer hiding but by revealing the following truths to God:

....

....

....

....

....

Shelter in the Storm

He who dwells in the shelter of the Most High will abide in the shadow of the Almighty. I will say to the LORD, "My refuge and my fortress, my God, in whom I trust."

~PSALM 91:1–2

One thing I can say for certain is we've all experienced a storm! During a storm, wouldn't you love to hunker down with a nice bowl of soup or watch a movie with a bag of popcorn, a slice of chocolate cake, or another comforting snack? There's so much outside your window to hear and see. The winds blow the rainwater, the thunder cracks the sky, and the lightning strikes! With all that going on outside, there you sit, bundled up in blankets and cozy socks, completely sheltered. Now hold that thought!

No matter what you're going through or what is going on around you, thankfully there is *always* shelter when you choose to abide in the Most High. God is your refuge and your sanctuary in the middle of the storm, if only you trust in him. Believe me, I know how hard it is to trust God at times! Every winter, I get the most painful acne on my face, and my energy takes a dive. I used to constantly complain about it. I'd spend a lot of time searching for the best winter skin care regimen and researching the underlying causes of low energy.

After years of unsuccessfully trying to "fix" myself, I decided the winter months were not the time for me to be the go-getter, full-speed-ahead social butterfly I was naturally in the spring and summer months. I decided that during the winter, I'd be like a bear, grateful to take this time to hibernate, abide more deeply in the shadows and shelter of God, and allow God to restore my energy, prepare my vessel, and order my steps at the appointed time.

Whatever the storms in your life may be—your health, your relationships, your child, your job—don't feel that you must quiet the storm on your own. Run to the shelter of the Lord. Create space in your life to have regular conversations with God. Allow God to be your refuge, and trust that his love and grace will see you through!

Heavenly Creator, thank you for being a hedge of protection around my life. Help me trust wholeheartedly that you will not allow the storms to overtake me but that you will always be my fortress, my refuge, and my shelter, even in the midst of the storm.

Today, with trust and gratitude, I take shelter in God by focusing on these good things:

....

....

....

....

....

In the Now You Have Won

*"And now why do you wait? Rise and be baptized
and wash away your sins, calling on his name."*

~ACTS 22:16

In this age of spiritual enlightenment, you may have heard about
the power of now. In my work as a spiritual advisor, I help my clients
experience the gift of the present moment by sharing what I refer to as
"divinity codes"—short and sweet, easy-to-remember words that can be
repeated or recalled in an instant, in order to activate God's universal laws
of love within you. The divinity code that illustrates the power of now is
this: When you are in the *now* you have *won* because you *own* it.

Did you notice that all three letters in the word *now* are used to form
the words *won* and *own*? Being in the now will allow you to win over your
circumstances because you are sitting with, or "owning," the love lessons
that the now is here to teach you. Thankfully, God is always right here,
right now! God is always in the *present*, which is another word for *gift*. This
means that fully surrendering to the now will allow you to connect with
the help of God to wash away your sins and be made new again. So take
a deep breath and come to the now. Why wait?

You will begin to make peace with the present moment when you
get still long enough to realize that God knew this moment, whatever
it is, would arrive. Before God gave you human life, this moment was
already written, or "*pre-sent*." Thank God! He knows exactly what
you're going through and what sin you might be entangled in. Rise
up. Do not delay! Surrender to the now by allowing it to be what it is.
Only then will you own it and win!

Heavenly Creator, I am grateful that I need not think about my past or my future, for I know the quality of my future is in direct proportion to how well I do now. I ask that you help me not resist all that the present moment presents to me. As I call upon your name, wash away my sins, baptize me, and make me new.

Today, I am grateful to receive the gift in the present moment, now. I will journal what comes to me:

....

....

....

....

....

Day 70

Amazing Grace

*For by grace you have been saved through faith.
And this is not your own doing; it is the gift of God,
not a result of works, so that no one may boast.*

~EPHESIANS 2:8–9

We are often taught in life that whenever something bad happens, there will be some form of punishment or consequence. Maybe when you were of school age, your parents scolded you for not getting the best grades on your report card. Perhaps you got into trouble whenever you didn't dress or act a certain way in public or at church. We often carry these high standards with us into adulthood, and when we mess up, as we all inevitably do, we find it increasingly difficult to forgive ourselves.

Some of us immediately rush to right our wrongs. Sadly, others of us believe that certain acts are unforgivable, that no matter what we do, we can never do enough to make things right. But no matter what we did, the truth in this moment is that it is done and cannot be undone. Thankfully, scripture assures us that grace does not come by way of our works, but by way of our faith. From Romans 11:6 we learn that grace would not be grace if works are required.

I've received so much grace in my life. I know that grace is real; without it, I would surely not be here, answering God's calling on my life today. Rest assured, your failures and imperfections are all necessary parts of your perfect walk with Christ!

No matter what you have done, and no matter what might have been done unto you to make you doubt that you can move forward, today I invite you to trust in God's word: "You have been saved by grace." The only work you must do is the work of staying in faith. Yes, I divorced, but I held fast to the faith that God's grace would give me another chance at love, and I was blessed to find my loving husband. Yes, I was raised in a religious belief system that caused me to question whether I was serving God in the "right way," but thankfully God's gifts of love, forgiveness, and grace remind me that I am his vessel each and every day.

Heavenly Creator, I may have been proven wrong in the eyes of another, and even in my own eyes at times, but I know that you always see me beyond my errors and mistakes. Today I will commit to following your instruction by reaching beyond my perceived errors, and holding fast to your amazing grace!

Today, with gratitude and thanks, I will receive God's free gift of grace having faith in this new possibility:

....

....

....

....

....

Crown On, Head High

But you, O LORD, are a shield around me; you are my
glory, the one who holds my head high.

~PSALM 3:3 NLT

Misogynistic messages abound in society. From the time we were little girls, many of us were taught either directly or indirectly that our value is based on how pretty or sweet we are. Collectively, there's been little to no acknowledgment of how intelligent we are. From lesser pay, to sexual harassment, to delayed civil rights, social institutions and practices have created the illusion that women are less than.

The war, destruction, sexual immorality, and greed you see in our world are in direct proportion to the imbalance of male and female energy. God is both masculine and feminine. *You* are the feminine energy of God. Do your part to bring about the balance by standing in the glory of God, which you were created to be. You are a warrior! Grab your shield, claim your crown, keep your head to the sky. Shine the beauty of your wisdom, love, and grace. Crown on. Head high!

Do not be afraid of man and twisted faces. Take no thought of their disgraces. You do not worship man; you worship our Almighty God! Ask, that you may receive. Forgive, that you may breathe! Trust the divinity within you. Press forward in the midst of your imperfections and apprehensions. Come as you are—you are worthy, you are protected, you are called! Our world needs you right now. You are the feminine energy of God.

Heavenly Creator, thank you for crowning me with your glory! Be a shield around me as I walk boldly into my divinity. Help me no longer look to the left or the right, seeking the approval of men, for I am a queen, created with a crown.

Today, I am grateful to stand in the glory of my divinity by being courageous in these areas of my life:

....

....

....

....

....

While Today Is Still Today

Jesus Christ is the same yesterday
and today and forever.

~HEBREWS 13:8

Whenever you feel unwell or at a loss, remember to stop, look lovingly within the depths of your soul, and call upon Jesus. But don't stop there. Listen to what Jesus instructs you to do. He will surely show you how to take a bad day and make it better, but you must be attuned to the people and circumstances that he is working through. Sometimes you'll find that turning your emotions around is as simple as giving thanks.

In every experience, good or bad, God is the same loving God *all day, every day*. So praise God while today is still today! The more you walk with Jesus, you'll find that life is not about what happened yesterday, nor is it about what might happen tomorrow. Life is about trusting and believing in God every step of the way. As a believer, what can you do to honor the presence of God in your life today? How can you change your thinking to show God you understand that there is joy not only in the destination but in the journey as well?

I start each day by acknowledging God and spending a few moments to express my gratitude. Thank you for my breath, my children, my family and friends, the warmth of my bed, and so on. I take it a step further by placing my slippers underneath may bed so that I must bend down and get on my knees, stopping to praise God and ask for direction before I take my very first step! Indeed, seeking first the kingdom of God can have a profound impact on the quality of your day, so don't leave home without him!

Try to see negative experiences in a new light. A late start means you got the extra rest that you needed. A long day at work shows you just how much you're needed. Ask yourself, "How would I respond to life's inconveniences if I knew Jesus was there through it all?" Act accordingly.

Heavenly Creator, thank you for your presence in my life today; and always. Thank you for being in the midst of the storms, and in the glory of my triumphs. Thank you for being a guiding light for my feet along the path you have laid out for me. Today, help me to not just walk, but frolic with heavenly bliss, joy, and glee!

Today, with gratitude, I stop, look, and listen to you. In these areas of life, you're guiding me through:

....

....

....

....

....

Day 73

Leave Your Past Behind

Brothers and sisters, I do not consider myself yet to have
taken hold of it. But one thing I do: Forgetting what is
behind and straining toward what is ahead, I press on
toward the goal to win the prize for which God has
called me heavenward in Christ Jesus.

~PHILIPPIANS 3:13–14 NIV

So often we make a habit of wasting precious moments in the present
by replaying scenes of our past actions. We can become so engulfed in
the memories of what we have done, as well as the wrongs we have
suffered, that we completely lose ourselves in the television show of our
life story. Thank God, we can turn the channel!

The past has influenced the person you are today, but the past itself
is done. Forgive the transgressions of others, as well as your own. Release
them to God and press forward toward the prize he has waiting for you!
Ask for forgiveness so you may receive the grace God has that is already
yours. I know it's hard to believe that God can be so forgiving, but he
knows that one of the devil's most common tactics is to tempt you to use
the pain of your past to keep you from your future. When you live backward, you are in the grips of the following divinity code found within the
reversed spelling of the words *live and lived*: When you *live* backward, you
experience *evil*.

We have all *lived* backward; therefore, we have all known the *devil*.
Leave your past behind! Press on toward the goal, to win the prize for
which God has called you heavenward in Christ Jesus.

Heavenly Creator, thank you for helping me fix my eyes not on the past but on you. In order to release my past, I am ready to forgive others as you have forgiven me. Whether it be drawing close or peacefully walking away, help me do all things in love.

Today, it is with gratitude and forgiveness that I seek God's help to release these painful parts of my past:

....

....

....

....

....

Day 74

Loving You

"Love the LORD with all your heart and with all your soul
and with all your mind and with all your strength.'
The second is this: 'Love your neighbor as yourself.'
There is no commandment greater than these."

~MARK 12:30–31

Love God with all your soul and mind and strength, and love your
neighbor as yourself. It never ceases to amaze me how many people mis-
understand what this commandment from Jesus really means. It is typical
for many to read this Scripture and think, *Sure, I love my neighbors. I wave, I
speak, and I share niceties and pleasantries at neighborhood gatherings. I'm nice to the
coffee shop employees. I engage in small talk with my coworkers. . . . I do this for that
person and that for this person.* The list goes on and on.

Women have been honing our natural ability to love others for
a long time. From the time we were little girls, we've been loving on
everything from our dolls to our stuffed animals to our younger siblings.
We've learned to take loving others to such an extreme that we often
forget to love ourselves!

Managing work and family life and providing emotional support to
others can truly take a toll on our hearts. This way of being causes us to
be highly susceptible to heartbreak—is it any wonder that heart disease
is the number one killer of women? With all the *doing* you do for other
people, add loving yourself to the top of the list.

Strive to live each day with the knowledge that you are worthy of God's love. In his eyes, you are perfect, and you honor him by loving yourself accordingly. Only then can you share with your neighbors the grace and compassion he has given to you through his eternal love. Begin today, and each day after, by greeting yourself with loving words before you invite the world in to receive his love through you.

Heavenly Creator, thank you for revealing to me that next to loving you, loving myself is my greatest priority! I know that the better I am to me, the better I'll be to others. Help me learn how to love me more deeply.

Today, I am grateful to love myself first, creating more time by setting the following boundaries in my life:

....

....

....

....

....

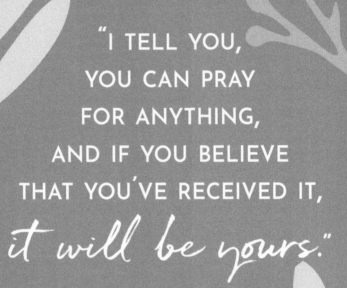

"I TELL YOU,
YOU CAN PRAY
FOR ANYTHING,
AND IF YOU BELIEVE
THAT YOU'VE RECEIVED IT,
it will be yours."

~MARK 11:24 NLT

Your Belief Will Be Life

For as long as I can remember, I longed for a few things. I wanted to heal from my physical and emotional pain. I wanted a personal relationship with God, and I wanted to help the world evolve to love. I truly had some wildly ambitious desires, yet I kept on believing. I believed with the faith of a tiny mustard seed, and I am grateful God gave me the desires of my heart.

Whatever you desire, pray for it, press for it, march forward for it— not looking to the left or the right for it! Ask and believe you have already received it, and it will be yours.

Heavenly Creator, thank you for giving me the very tangible tools for achieving the desires you have placed within my heart. I have asked; now I will believe. Help me be filled with joy, peace, and gratitude as if it were already received.

Today, it is with a grateful heart that I hold the following positive beliefs about my life:

....

....

....

....

Day 76

Are You Listening?

Understand this, my dear brothers and sisters:
You must all be quick to listen, slow to speak,
and slow to get angry.

~JAMES 1:19 NLT

There is a reason God created us with two ears and one mouth. By our very design, we were created to listen twice as much as we speak. Have you ever been in a conversation with someone and found yourself so busy formulating what you were going to say when the person finished talking that you didn't hear what they said at all?

Disagreements arise when either person believes their way is the most logical way to view or address any given situation. Thankfully, resolutions are quick to come by when we learn to listen twice as much as we speak. This is why God says, "Be slow to speak and quick to listen." I caution you, there is a difference between listening and hearing. We hear with our ears but listen with our heart. Be aware of the difference to protect yourself from being angry.

The next time you find yourself in a conversation that starts to go in a negative direction, don't get so caught up in what you're going to say or how you're going to prove your point or get the other person to understand your logic. Just stop, listen from your heart, and try to truly connect with what the other person is trying to express to you. Rather than reacting in anger, you will surely gain the insight and awareness you need by responding with love.

Heavenly Creator, I am grateful to understand the importance of listening more and speaking less. Give me the strength to bite my tongue in the heat of the moment, for your word says that it is not what goes into a person's mouth that defiles them but what comes out. Guard my mouth, and help me listen from the heart, that I may speak words rooted in resolution, gratitude, peace, and love.

Today, I am grateful to be quick to listen and slow to speak when interacting with the following people:

....

....

....

....

....

Just Do It

*"Arise, for it is your task, and we are with you;
be strong and do it."*

~EZRA 10:4

One famous footwear and sportswear brand has amassed a net worth of billions of dollars, largely due to its symbolic swoosh and a marketing slogan that tugs at our soul's deepest desire—to "just do it." The brand experts must have known that too many of us don't do the things we want to do because of the gazillion reasons we can think of for why not to.

I could go to the gym today, but it's raining. I should write that book, but I just don't think I can handle traveling back through that pain. What will people think about me? Someone might get offended. I could apply for a new job, but what if I never hear back? What if I'm ridiculed? I really want to leave this relationship, this dead-end job, but where will I go? Forget all the what-ifs and just do it!

The journey of a brave and successful woman of God is this: She proceeds in the midst of the fear, the doubt, the adversity, and the pain. She calls upon the help of the Lord, and, come what may, she just does it! Can you imagine where our world would be if our most inspiring female role models didn't just do it? Where would our world be if *you* just did it, too?

When you see yourself on the edge of life's virtual cliffs of uncertainty, don't stand there looking over, terrified and afraid to fall. Take the leap of faith—jump! Just do it. When you are willing to risk falling, that's when you'll grow your wings, take off, and fly. Swoosh! Mount up on the wings of the heavenly host that will surely come to your aid when you *just do* all that God has called you to.

Heavenly Creator, thank you for giving me the spiritual strength and internal fortitude to just do it! Help me not be worried or ashamed of my weakness, for it is in my weakness that I am made stronger in you.

Today, with boldness, gratitude, and God on my side, I will *just do it* in these areas of my life:

....

....

....

....

....

Day 78

Be an Uplifter!

*But encourage one another daily, as long
as it is called "Today," so that none of you
may be hardened by sin's deceitfulness.*

~HEBREWS 3:13 NIV

Perhaps at some point today you will encounter someone who is not
warm to you. You might take it personally as a calculated attack, but
don't be deceived by sin's deceitfulness.

Whenever a person appears closed off, distant, or has a bad attitude,
remember this has nothing to do with you. Their outward behavior is a
reflection of their inner state of being. What *is* within your power is the
ability to offer the love and encouragement they may not be aware they
are seeking. When you do, you are spreading God's love—and thankfully
there's plenty to share because it's infinite!

I'll never forget an experience I had with my local barista. On most
days, she'd greet me with a bright and welcoming smile. When I was
writing my first book, I'd talked about it with her, and she expressed
genuine excitement to read it. One day, God put it in my heart to gift my
book to her once it had published.

The day that I arrived at the coffee shop with my just-published book,
I met a very different version of my barista. She did not greet me with
her smile and she made no eye contact. Right away, I began to question
the authenticity of her past behaviors as I searched for an explanation.
I grabbed my coffee, sat down, and proceeded to pray. God asked me,
"Are you going to love this woman without conditions?"

I immediately grabbed her attention and asked her to come see me
when she had a break. She did, and when I handed her my book, she

lit up with her typical bright light. She was so very thankful! As her shift went on, I could tell by the change in her personality that our interaction was just the encouragement she needed to get her out of the temporary funk she'd been in.

Whenever I'm in a funk, I find someone I can call, uplift and encourage. It not only helps them to feel better, it helps me to feel better too. Encouraging another person is a great and highly effective way to shift your focus from "Woe is me" to gratitude.

Heavenly Creator, help me be an encourager every day. Help me seize the opportunity to lift someone up by acknowledging their accomplishments or offering a gesture of love in the form of a compliment or good deed. May my encouraging words be a healing balm to the hearts of the hardened or afflicted, keeping us both united, uplifted, and free from sin's deceitfulness.

Today, it is with a heart of gratitude that I lovingly encourage and uplift these persons in these ways:

....

....

....

....

....

Feel It to Heal It

"I have said these things to you, that in me you may have peace. In the world you will have tribulation. But take heart; I have overcome the world."

~JOHN 16:33

It is only human to experience a range of emotions as we move through this life. It's easy for our minds to get preoccupied with all matters of the heart, but how often do we stop to truly connect with how our painful experiences have defined who we now are? And how often do we reflect on whether we are capable of getting past the pain of earlier experiences?

Maybe, like me, you have lived through many deeply painful experiences. Maybe a single betrayal or painful encounter has stayed with you over the course of years. It's hard to comprehend why or how people can cause one another such pain. We may never be able to answer these questions for ourselves, and there's never going to be a good reason. That's why focusing on the people who have hurt us will lead only to anger, frustration, and lack of forgiveness. Instead, remember that those who have caused you pain were in the midst of losing their own battle between the flesh and the spirit.

Ask God to give you a heart of forgiveness, and shift your focus to how you can heal. How do you feel about yourself, the people around you, and your life as a consequence of your painful experiences? Cry about it. Talk to God about the negative thoughts, beliefs, and behaviors those painful seeds have caused to take root in you. This is the surest pathway to your peace.

You cannot change what you do not acknowledge. You cannot heal what you do not allow yourself to feel. Find a person you trust and can talk to, and bring your trials and tribulations to God! Your freedom is on the other side of taking heart and having the courage to understand just who you are.

Heavenly Creator, thank you for being my refuge, my safe haven, and my peace. Help me travel boldly through my deepest feelings with the intention of healing. Help me open my heart to forgiveness, that I may use my trials and tribulations to glorify you.

Today, it is with gratitude and self-love that I take these truest truths and deepest feelings to God for healing:

....

....

....

....

....

Day 80

Find the Light

"You will forget your misery; it will be like water flowing
away. Your life will be brighter than the noonday.
Even darkness will be as bright as morning."

~JOB 11:16–17 NLT

It's not what we experience in life that has the greatest impact; it's
how we respond to it. Perspective is everything! By its very definition,
perspective refers to having a particular attitude or way of regarding
something—a point of view. Do you think God wants you to view life's
obstacles through a lens of positivity or negativity?

Ask God in prayer, "What truths would I see if I looked upon this challenge with love and gratitude?" It is in moments of perceived darkness that
we have some of the greatest opportunities to seek and find the light!

For a long time, I resisted the temporary disease in my body that was
symptomatic of TMJ, a jaw joint disorder. The condition didn't just affect
the right side of my jawline; it also flowed down the right side of my neck,
shoulder, and upper back. It quickly began to interfere with my ability to
engage in activities of daily living, and I kept begging God to take it away.

One day while in prayer, I asked God to help me find the good this condition had to offer. God helped me realize some undeniable truths, which I
could not refute. Prior to developing the condition, it seemed I was always
in a rush. No matter where I was going, I hustled. TMJ slowed me down; I
could no longer move at a frantic pace. The pain prevented me from getting
ahead of myself. By slowing down, even in physical discomfort I began to
feel more peace in the relative stillness of my environment. The condition
kept me grounded and prevented me from taking on anything beyond my
mental, emotional, and spiritual capacity.

When our perspective evolves, we evolve. Our resistance diminishes. We all have an opportunity to see the light in the darkness. How can you see your experience as a gift? No matter how dark the darkness may appear, prayer and gratitude will always lead you to the light!

Heavenly Creator, thank you for your power to turn darkness into light! Help me walk with a posture of boldness, courage, and gratitude through the dark places in my life. Even the darkness will be as morning, for I will surely see the light.

Today, I am grateful to let darkness fall behind me as I brighten my perspective in the light of the Son:

....

....

....

....

....

Whom Shall I Fear?

The LORD is my light and my salvation;
whom shall I fear? The LORD is the stronghold
of my life; of whom shall I be afraid?

~PSALM 27:1

Do you recall having been afraid of the dark when you were little? Picture yourself at five years old. You're lying in your bed, and the lights are out. You have the covers pulled up to your eyes as you peek over at your dresser. You lay there frozen and afraid, wondering if there's a monster in your room. Then, you decide to jump out of bed, run over, and turn on the lights! You breathe a deep sigh of relief when you realize the darkness is *gone*, and it was just your teddy bear sitting there.

How long have you sat there procrastinating in life, paralyzed by fear? Perhaps you've heard the saying, "F.E.A.R. is false evidence appearing real." Take a few moments to consider if this statement is true for you. Reflect on the thoughts that cause you to feel worry, anxiety, and fear. Have those fears come true? Eight times out of 10, probably not. In fact, scientific research reveals that 80 to 90 percent of our thoughts never actually come true!

For most of my life, I was afraid of everything! Even if there was nothing to be afraid of, I made something up to fear—"What if I don't make it to the school bus on time and something happens to my child?" "What if this ingrown hair is not an ingrown hair but a sign of disease?" "What if he's lying or cheating?" And I bet you have your own list of fears, but why? Fear not!

Whenever fearful thoughts threaten to flood your mind, replace them with thoughts of truth, and make a conscious decision not to give worry any credit 'til it's due. Instead, speak over yourself by declaring, "The Lord is my strength and my salvation. Whom shall I fear?"

Heavenly Creator, thank you for being my strength and my helper. Help me release thoughts of worry, anxiety, and fear to you by walking through my life carrying the flashlight of your love and my truth.

Today, I am grateful to release "false evidence appearing real" by thinking on these things in love and in truth:

....

....

....

....

....

Climb Every Mountain

"Every valley shall be filled in, every mountain
and hill made low. The crooked roads shall
become straight, the rough ways smooth."

~LUKE 3:5 NIV

From the time you couldn't pay your bill to the time it was paid in full. From the time you couldn't leave that toxic friendship to the time you actually did. From the many times you've fallen to the many times you've gotten up. Stop for a moment and give God thanks and praise for every mountain he's brought you over!

Scripture tells us so much about what God can do when we allow him to help us through. God said the valleys will be filled with the light and the glory of the Lord—his rod and staff are with you. You know those visions, dreams, hills, and glorious mountaintops that seem too high to climb? God has the power to bring them down low enough for you to reach. With his strength, you will run and not faint! Every crooked place—God will make it straight! Even the rough places will be made smooth. This is what God wants to do for you!

You will never have to climb the mountains alone. Invite God to walk with you over every mountain, and praise him for every valley he's already seen you through. Thank God in the highest praise for every blessing, and watch how quickly he will make your bumpy roads smooth!

*Heavenly Creator, I give you glory and the highest
praise for every hill you have made low in my life.
Thank you for placing mountaintops within my
reach. I give my crooked places to you, that you
would make them straight. May my life be a walking
testimony of the blessings that come when we trust
your word and accept your grace!*

**Today, I am grateful to reflect with gratitude on the
mountains and the valleys God has already brought
me through:**

....

....

....

....

....

Day 83

Keep the Faith

And without faith it is impossible to please him, for
whoever would draw near to God must believe that
he exists and that he rewards those who seek him.

~HEBREWS 11:6

Is one of your greatest desires to please God? We are so fortunate
that God rewards those who seek him. The Bible says, "Many are the
afflictions of the righteous, but the LORD delivers him out of them all"
(Psalm 34:19). When we feel our earthly needs and wants are fulfilled,
our gratitude abounds, but what about when we don't get what we
want? Do you still have faith that you will earn the kingdom of God
even as you ride the waves of daily life?

The Bible describes "faith" as the assurance of things hoped for
and the conviction of things not seen. When I left my well-paid corpo-
rate job and started a ministry to help others understand Jesus better,
the Spirit instructed me not to associate myself with any particular
religious affiliation; it was my faith that caused me to be obedient to
God's calling. Today, I serve God's children from various religious
backgrounds. I believe it was God who gave me the dream, and the
rewards for my faith continue to flow to me.

Some of the biggest barriers to faith are fear and disbelief in ourselves. Activate your faith by doing the things you fear you cannot do and
even the things for which some might try to ridicule you. Regardless of
the form the adversity might take, always do your best to keep the faith!

Fear will scream at you in its loud and ornery voice, "Impossible!" While faith will whisper to you gently, "I'm possible!" Same words, yet faith provides you an encouraging perspective and a whole lot of grace! Your faith doesn't demand that you finish everything you set out to accomplish; it simply asks that you walk through the doors.

Heavenly Creator, thank you for making my walk with you simplified by faith. When the feelings get heavy and the road is not so bright, thank you for helping me walk by faith and not by sight. In whatever form it might take, I know that my reward will inevitably be the experience of your bright light!

Today, I am grateful to walk by faith, believing with assurance that God will help me accomplish these things in my life:

....

....

....

....

....

Day 84

The Gift of Gratitude

*Every good gift and every perfect gift is from above,
coming down from the Father of lights, with whom
there is no variation or shadow due to change.*

~JAMES 1:17

Every good and perfect gift comes from the Lord. Our challenges come from the Lord as well. You are at the top of the list of God's good and perfect gifts. You are the *light* that the Father of lights created! And, thankfully, God's love for you does not vary due to the shadows and changes in your life.

Think back to a time when you experienced dark clouds, then recall the blessing that came when the clouds cleared and the sunshine set in. It's amazing how the things we fear will take us out often become things for which we can be grateful. Yes, my first marriage ended, but instead of focusing on what went wrong, I choose to remember and be grateful for the good gifts with which the relationship blessed me—namely, our beautiful son. It may seem unfortunate that I developed a chronic jaw joint and ligament condition shortly after a minor car accident, but thank God! That fender bender brought me to my knees, which was the catalyst for me turning my life over to Christ.

The miracle of gratitude is that it looks upon every situation from a higher altitude, always seeking the light, even when the gift of the experience is hidden within the darkness. God wants to bless you, even in the shadows of your life, and in fact has blessed you already *if you only choose to acknowledge it*. So thank God today and every day, and just watch how much more you'll have to be thankful for!

Heavenly Creator, help me experience the gift of gratitude by taking a few moments to thank you for all things that happen in my life each day. Thank you for allowing me to do it and healing me through it. Thank you for being the light that shines away my shadows. I am grateful that although seasons change, your love for me remains the same.

Today, I will experience the gift of gratitude by seeing these situations with love, from a higher altitude:

....

....

....

....

....

Day 85

A Miracle in Store

"Seek the Kingdom of God above all else, and live
righteously, and he will give you everything you need."

~MATTHEW 6:33 NLT

There's no denying that, like many others, I was devastated when the world lost Whitney Houston. To her fans, God's light shined through her, and her beautiful voice penetrated the depths of our souls, connecting us with the very vibrations of love! I am so grateful for the lasting gifts she brought to us through her music.

In the wake of her death, I listened to one song she had sung called "Miracle." It particularly spoke to my soul. It seemed to give insight into her very own soul's cry as she lamented a deep regret. The lyrics spoke to her carelessness with what she calls a miracle, and the challenge of facing every day after casting it off. Whitney goes on to sing of choosing love and how, in making that choice, another miracle may be in store.

Nothing should matter but the voice of love. Not fortune, not fame, not even accolades—focusing on these things can be the very cause of downfall and distraction from God's love. To seek and choose love is to seek and choose God. Seek first the kingdom of God, and all things will be added unto you.

To have all things yet not hold on to God is to throw away a miracle. Don't throw away your miracle; when the challenges come, and they do, hold on tightly to God's love, and keep striving to live righteously, allowing him to bring you to new and higher heights. Trust and believe there's a miracle in store for you!

Heavenly Creator, thank you for being all I need in order to succeed! From the healing of my body and the cleansing of my soul to the reaching of my goals, thank you in advance for the miracle in store.

Today, I am grateful to seek first the kingdom of God by focusing on living righteously in these ways:

....

....

....

....

....

Stillness Is a Stretch

"Be still, and know that I am God. I will be exalted
among the nations, I will be exalted in the earth!"

~PSALM 46:10

Don't you find it interesting that to get to know God, all we have to do is be still? This seems like it should be a cakewalk, but you and I both know how far that is from the truth! It seems with all our doing, we have forgotten how to just *be*. Even when we're just being, are we being with God or the TV, the laptop, the smartphone, or any other distraction? You might be physically still, but your mind is racing 100 miles per hour as it takes in the energy—good or bad—of all that you are absorbing through your senses.

Stillness asks that you close your eyes and go within to visit the residence of your soul, where God resides. Look at nature and notice that all things exalt God with stillness and movement and grace. Birds fly with ease and flow, as if in no hurry to get anywhere. Trees sway gently with the wind, never out of step with the dance, and horses graze silently and peacefully, keeping one another pleasant company.

I know you desire very much to feel for yourself the presence and power of God in stillness. With all you have going on, making time for being still might sound like a stretch. What if I told you it *is* a stretch? It is, but a different kind of stretch. You will be fascinated by how many deep conversations you'll have with God when you take just five minutes a day to turn on some soft, melodic music, get down on the ground, close your eyes, and simply stretch into your being.

I say you need only five minutes because I know the moment you start stretching, it'll feel so good, and your conversation with God will be so profound, you won't think five minutes is nearly enough time. In that case, stay as long as you need! Savor your stillness, and when you emerge back into your day, you will be in a state of awe and gratitude about how your body, your eating habits, your mental health, your courage, and your clarity will rise to meet you!

Heavenly Creator, thank you for teaching me the importance of stillness. Help me make time with you a necessary part of my day, like brushing my teeth or combing my hair. I am grateful for the guidance that stillness with you will bring to me.

Today, with deep gratitude, I commit to spending five minutes with God while stretching and conversing about:

....

....

....

....

....

Day 87

Silence Speaks Volumes

"The LORD will fight for you, and
you have only to be silent."

~EXODUS 14:14

Has someone ever made you so mad that all you wanted to do was give them a piece of your mind and tell them where you were coming from and where they needed to go? I'm not talking about the kind of mad you get when you get served cold fries at McDonald's or when your manager requests you do a last-minute report you hadn't planned to do. I'm talking about the kind of angry that happens when someone does something that cuts you to the core.

Usually only those closest to us can ever get us this angry. While it is always healthy to express ourselves, there comes a time when silence speaks more loudly than words. If you are ever in a disagreement with someone and it starts to get out of hand, let this be your cue that it is time to get quiet and allow the Lord to fight for you.

Anger is sadness that has not had a chance to express itself. Your silence will allow the other person time to reflect on their own actions and behaviors while also giving you the opportunity to look beyond your anger to connect with what's really hurting you. Allow God to speak to you in the silence. He will tell you exactly how to handle the matter with love, and the battle will be won, without you having to fight at all!

Heavenly Creator, I am grateful to know that I can hang up my boxing gloves and allow you to fight my battles for me! Help me allow myself to be not with the anger but with the sadness that another person may have helped me connect with. I hand the matter to you, for your gracious resolution to shine through.

Today, I am grateful to release myself from anger and resentment by giving these people to God in silence and prayer:

....

....

....

....

....

Day 88

How You See It

If any of you lacks wisdom, you should ask God,
who gives generously to all without finding
fault, and it will be given to you.
~JAMES 1:5 NIV

Wouldn't you just love to have the answer to all of your questions in life? It's easy to become consumed with knowing the why and when of our experiences.

I have experienced my fair share of situations that left me questioning whether God listened to my prayers. I've learned to rely on God over the years because no matter how long I have had to wait, in the end he always showed up and showed out!

What if God is working the most when you see him the least? What if that dry season you're experiencing right now is merely a test of your faith? No matter what the challenge may be, passing the test is all about how you see it. Will you choose positivity or negativity? From Matthew 11:28–30, we know that Jesus said, "My yoke is easy, and my burden is light." Perhaps those times we feel heaviest is when we think we can solve our problems without seeking the wisdom of God.

It is such a relief to know that when you are unsure of how to deal with certain things, all you have to do is ask. In his own way, God will generously provide you with the wisdom and understanding you need to proceed. You might even feel a prompting to just *wait*, in which case you move on by waiting on the Lord!

I have struggled with and overcome many fears about my finances, health, husband, children, health, and even my relationship with myself. When I decided to stop blaming myself and everyone else for everything,

I was able to ask God to give me the insight to see it differently. Changing your perspective can take you from feeling as though you're going *nowhere* to a feeling that no matter what, you are *now here*, and that's perfectly ok!

The exact same letters are used in the words "nowhere" and "now here." The difference lies only in how you choose to see it. Thankfully, you have the power to ask for and receive the gift of a positive perspective. I guarantee, when you change your thoughts, you will inevitably change your life.

Heavenly Creator, thank you for helping me to see my life through the lens of wisdom, and help me to respond accordingly. Teach me to trust in the power of your word, as you generously pour out your holy spirit upon me. Help me to wait on and trust in you, for I know you are with me in all I experience and all that I do.

Today, with deep surrender and a heart of gratitude, I will look for the light shining through this situation:

....

....

....

....

....

Day 89

The Spirit and the Law

Let me ask you only this: Did you receive the Spirit
by works of the law or by hearing with faith?

~GALATIANS 3:2

As a young girl, my first glimpse of God came through the teachings of the Jehovah's Witnesses religion. As I grew older, I found it very difficult to adopt many of their ideologies about the rules and rituals one needed to follow as a show of belief in the one true Jehovah, or God.

In my next stop along the path to God, I joined a local Baptist church. I thoroughly enjoyed the Sunday services, and I served as a Sunday school teacher. I felt comfortable enough with my church family to share my struggles. I was heartbroken when the pastor himself took advantage of my unhealed wounds and weaknesses.

When I asked God to reveal the truth about who he is, I received a strong prompting to study the life of Jesus Christ. If Jesus had followed the laws of the religious men of his time, he would not have healed on the Sabbath day, and he would not have allowed the man who didn't follow with him to cast out demons in his name. He would not have spared the stoning of the woman caught in adultery, and he would not have called himself a god, which was the alleged blasphemy for which these men of the law had him put to death (John 10:33).

We may at times question the practices of our churches, but the life and example of Jesus Christ never ceases to thrill my heart and propel me forward. My study of the Bible connects me with the love, peace, healing, and grace of God. Do you too feel that you are in a safe place when you throw yourself into the words of our Savior? If anyone in your congregation causes you to remain in guilt, shame, or judgment of yourself and others, turn your attention inward. Follow the guidance of the Holy Spirit, and have faith that your internal guide is true. When in doubt, lean in to the Holy Spirit, who is not susceptible to the weaknesses of humanity.

Heavenly Creator, thank you for prompting me to be a listener of the Holy Spirit within me. Help me hear the Spirit and receive all things with faith, for I know my faith will help me finish the eternal race that leads me home to you!

Today, I am grateful to sit in silence and receive these instructions from God through the Holy Spirit with faith:

....

....

....

....

....

"YOU DID NOT CHOOSE ME, BUT

AND APPOINTED YOU THAT

YOU SHOULD GO AND BEAR

FRUIT AND THAT YOUR FRUIT

SHOULD ABIDE, SO THAT

WHATEVER YOU ASK THE

FATHER IN MY NAME,

HE MAY GIVE IT TO YOU."

~JOHN 15:16

Day 90
Say Yes

God chose you. Will you choose God? Today say yes! Say yes to your dreams. Say yes to facing your fears. Say yes to the beautiful, glorious temple of God you see—or are still striving to see—when you look in the mirror. Why not? What good is resisting going to do? Recognize that the only way to dive ever deeper in faith, to experience the gifts God has in store for you, is to say yes to both the known and unknown.

Isn't it amazing to accept that God chose and appointed you to bear good fruit at such a time as this? Today, say yes to your calling, even if you're called to give yourself rest. Say yes to yourself; in doing so, may you become ever more aware of his glory working in you.

Heavenly Creator, help me to move past the roadblocks that have caused me to say no in the past. Thank you for giving me the power and the courage to say yes! I am grateful to know that to say yes to me is to say yes to you.

Today, it is with gratitude that I plant new seeds and bear new fruit by saying yes to these dreams:

....

....

....

Verse Index

Old Testament

New Testament

About the Author

Sabrina U. Lawton is the founder of Evolve to Love, a spiritual advising organization. She credits her ability to have overcome a number of painful and even traumatic life experiences to believing God's word, embodying God's love, and finding gratitude in all things.

Sabrina is dedicated to helping believers from all over the world evolve in their personal relationships with God by sharing the power of love through the teachings of Jesus Christ. She is deeply passionate about helping God's children win the war between the flesh and the spirit, and humbly does so through keynote speaking engagements and writings.

Above all things, Sabrina is most grateful to enjoy the fruit of God's promises in her life, including her loving husband, Eric, and two beautiful children, Martin and Savannah.

Learn more at www.EvolveToLove.com.